To Becky
Best Wishes,
Simon Golding

Through
the Net

The Volleyball Memoirs of Simon Golding

PART ONE

Copyright Simon Golding and Otter Publications 2000

First Published in 2000 by **Otter Publications**,
9 Roman way, Fishbourne, Chichester, PO19 3QN.

ISBN 1 899053 16 6

Acknowledgements

I would like to thank all the hundreds of players that have supported my
various journalistic efforts over the years. Your kind words and encouragement have directly resulted in this book being written. Above and
beyond the call of duty I call it, not only did Tristan play a beach season
with me, but he also designed this book.Thanks also to Ann Johnson for
editing the book and providing me with some carefully worded advice.
Big shout to Starsk though. Everyone should have a mate like Starsk.
Thanks for all your help mate.

Photographs
Barabara Totterdell
Chris Hykiel
Simon Golding

Editor
Ann Johnson

Graphic Design
Tristan Boyd

Printed and bound in Great Britain.

The Otter Publications logo is reproduced from original artwork by
David Kitt.

Contents

For Freddie and Campbell.

Career Calculations

Total Playing years = 15

October 1985 - October 2000

Total Teams = 13

West Sussex Inst. (Sussex league) 1985 - 1990
Sussex Nomads (Div. 3 NVL) 1987 - 88
Capital City (Div.1 NVL) 1988 - 1990
Sheppey Spikers (Kent league) 1988 - 1989
Purbrook Portsmouth (Div.1 NVL) 1990 - 1991
Hastings CSSC (Sussex league) 1992 - 1995
Polonia (Div.1 NVL) 1991 - 1992 and 1998 - 1999
Wessex (Div.1 NVL) 1992, 1997 and 1999 - present
Solent (Div.1, 2, 3 NVL) 1992 - 1996 and 1997 - 1998
Thames Valley Jets (Div.2 NVL) 1996 - 1997
Dolphins (Southampton league) 1997 - 1998

Total Rep.Teams = 7

Great Britain Students, GB Civil Service, British Colleges squad, Sussex county, Kent county, Hampshire Allstars, SG Furnace Ambassadors.

Total International teams played = 16

Switzerland, Lithuania, Lativia, Denmark (Jnr), Scotland, England, Wales, N.Ireland, Repulic of Ireland, Germany, Turkey, America, Poland, Belgium, South Korea and Indonesia.

Total Beach Partners = 6

Neil Withington 1992
Julian Banasiewicz 1993 and 1994
Jurek Jankowski 1995
Steve Draper 1996 and 1997
Clayton Lucas 1998 and 1999
Chris Hykiel 1999 (Newquay, tournament cancelled)
Tristan Boyd 2000

Playing Achievements

World Student Games 1991
3 British Championship Bronze medals (1989, 1990, 1991)
2 EVA National Finals runners-up medals (1992, 2000)
EVA Super Cup runner-up (1992)
NVL Divison 1 runner-up (2000)
NVL Divison 3 South winners (1993, 1998)
NVL Div.3 South 'Player of the Year' (1993, 1998)
Beach Volleyball Grand Prix event winner (Poole 2000)
British Beach Volleyball Championships runner-up (2000)
8 Beach Volleyball Grand Prix runners-up medals (1993 - 2000)
Southwark Invitational winners(1998)
Brighton Invitational winners (2000)
Barry Island runners-up (2000)
Spirit of the Grand Prix (1992)
Scottish Indoor Open runners-up medal (1990)
BCSA Gold (1988)
Whitfield runners-up medals (1990, 1991)
3 Sussex Cup winners medals (1987, 1996, 1997)
4 Sussex Cup runners-up medals (1986, 1993, 1994, 1995)
3 Sussex League titles (1995, 1997, 1998)

Introduction

' Through the Net' is not a true historical record, simply an attempt to capture the spirit of a sport that has enthralled me and occupied a proportion of my thoughts for almost every single day of the last fifteen years of my life. To date I have read many interesting books on the sport, but never one which really reflects anything close to my experiences from season to season. I hope this book goes some way towards doing that for some of you.

I'm writing this at 12.50pm on a warm August day in London, sat on a brick wall outside the High Commission to Botswana off Bond street, of all places. The reason I'm here killing time is because I showed up to a television studio in St. Johns Wood at 11.00am (oohh! get me) to record a programme. They, the T.V moguls, told me that the programme had hit a production snag, usually code for it's not finished yet and would I turn up again at 2.00pm, usually code for 4.00pm. So with three hours to kill, minimum, I'm wandering around Central London looking in shops, watching interesting characters going about their business and pondering the pleasant fact that there aren't many jobs where you can get so well paid for simply hanging around and relaxing.

The television work has been fun and is fast becoming a career opportunity, something to fall back on if, and I mean if, Spielberg decides not to immortalise my volleyball career on celluloid.

I have recently been travelling up to London to record some beach volleyball shows, that aired on Channel 4. One studio I visited is the base for a lot of Disney Channel programmes. Only a few weeks ago I arrived at the studio to find a cluster of teenage girls eagerly awaiting the arrival of a boy band, I was pleasantly amused to be mistaken for band member and semi-mobbed. Semi-mobbing is the practised art of mobbing someone in case they are famous, but with enough restraint to withdraw from the melee with ease should non-fame be established. I ironically inquired of the twenty or so young girls whether the boy band they were waiting for were called 'ugly, fat and old ?' the only boy band I could conceivably have joined. The girls didn't do irony though. They all gave me that hideous, belittling teenage sneer that so many young adults use, when intellectually outclassed, to re-establish the status quo. It appeared the band were actually called something else, 'sub-zero', 'bodyheat', 'Nob-out' or some other startlingly original media creation.

My other brush with stardom ended in distinctly different circumstances. I had just finished recording a show in Camden Town, at a small studio close to where the MTV programmes are made. On walking back to the tube station I was conscious of a group of young ladies behind me making various comments.

"That's that bloke off MTV."

"It's him, that presenter bloke....you know."

I kept looking around me surreptitiously to see if I could spot the MTV star, no one stood out. I got to the escalator at Camden Tube Station and the young ladies were still behind me.

"Oi! MTV bloke, we know it's you." They kept saying.

I walked onto the platform and they surrounded me, not a semi-mob this time, a full mob. They thrust booklets, programmes and bits of paper in my direction.

"Sign this, it's got to say 'to Kylie, you're the bomb.'"

I protested that I was not who they thought I was. Initially I refused to sign, but they were clearly not going to leave me alone. So I patiently scrawled what they asked for then, where the signature went, I signed an unreadable line of pen with a couple of bumps strategically placed. They left me alone and seemed completely happy with the autograph of a man who wasn't the bloke that they thought I was off MTV, who's name they couldn't remember.

That kind of sums it up. Domestically, I have been near the top of my sport for a number of years, in relative anonymity and have received more notoriety walking innocently through London minding my own business, than in fifteen years of volleyball.

We are involved with the sport because we are motivated mostly by ourselves to be involved and that must make the game and the people we play alongside special.

So, why write this book? Surely my career when compared to the likes of Karch Kiraly, Beckham or a Spice Girl doesn't warrant a published testament to it's passing. In those terms of course it doesn't, although I have played for fifteen years, represented sixteen teams and played in every court position at the top domestic level both indoor and beach.

I have tried to justify this book in two ways. Firstly, writing a book is another one of those 'tick it off the list of things to do in life'. Secondly, my career has run concurrently with thousands of other volleyball players so the book aims to recount some of the experiences of a collective body of people who have devoted so much time and effort to this sport. That seemed a reasonable justification in itself.

The title? Well, 'Through the Net' was an article I used to write for the national magazine between 1992 - 94. It refers to the phenomena that occurs in many sports, namely players having a go at each other. Volleyballer's when they do have a go have to do it through the net. Besides that, I'm hoping to boost sales with some misguided purchases from computer enthusiasts.

My stories and my experiences will reflect many that you have encountered. In my own way I have achieved a number of things in volleyball that I am tremendously proud, both as a player and as a coach. Writing this book has proved to be a remarkably cathartic experience, enabling me to re-visit many distant, but surprisingly vivid, memories. Helping me to start to draw a line under my playing days. True it probably isn't my last swing on a volleyball court, I'm sure I will still play at various events over the years. But, as a competitive animal able to 'cut the mustard' at the top level in this country my time is strictly limited, 'cutting the cheese' is far more my style these days.

I have tried to write about events that happened in a vague chronological order, student volleyball, national league and finally the beach. Inevitably, with time, my stories may have been embellished here and there. You may read about yourself and have no recollection of ever saying or doing any of the things you are credited with, forgive me if that is the case. I used to say 'so sue me' in magazine editorials, but in today's litigious climate and with my tenuous grasp of the facts I fear that would be a little foolhardy.

To help you with the text I have included a bunch of photographs in the middle. To get you thinking about exactly where you were when I am referring to particular times in my career I have included a table of dates and things I did at those times.

The language is strong in places and the occasional situation coarse and lewd, but that is how it sometimes is. I apologise sincerely to the people who will read this book and don't always enjoy that kind of talk.

My final word of introduction concerns my desire not to cause offence to anyone mentioned in this book. Any person included within these pages is there because they influenced my volleyball career. Even if my experiences playing volleyball with those people were mixed, their effect on me helped me learn and develop as a player and coach and I'll always be grateful for that.

I take my hat off to all of you that play, coach, officiate, spectate and administrate a sport. Good luck to all of you with your future endeavours. I hope you enjoy the book.

It remains for me to thank the following people and dedicate this book to them, my reasons for mentioning each one will hopefully become apparent as you read on. There is no particular order to the list.

My wife Freddie, my parents (Jane and John, Denis and Pat) and Grandparents for all their love, help, encouragement and support. My kid brother Oliver for all his driving me around the country and for listening to hours and hours of bloody volleyball stories. Pat and Mike Withington, for making me so welcome in 1989. Nick and Carole Smith, for their friendship, encouragement and enthusiasm. Thanks Nick, for teaching me to play this great game and being such a positive influence on me. Phil Allen, for his all his work, patience and advice. Barbara Totterdell, for her fantastic photographic work and for all her support of my various journalistic schemes over the years. Mo Glover and Audrey Cooper, for giving me an opportunity to coach on the World Series. Fergus Leslie, Sava Medonos, Simon Coleman, Neil Withington, Dave and Della Gander, Stuart Dunne, Chris Hykiel, Clayton Lucas, Steve Draper, Julian Banasiewicz, Jurek Jankowski, Gary Duncan, Graham Sault, Keith Nicholls, Mike Rhodes, Grant Pursey, Richard Cannon, Geoff and Lynn Allen, Tristan Boyd, Starsk and Dom all for various bits of help too numerous to mention.

Chapter 1
The College Years, where it all began

The current state of nearly no play...............

The NHS consultant gave it to me straight. I had known him for around three minutes. Three minutes in which he had repeated exactly the same manipulations of my right leg that my GP had performed weeks earlier. He approached his task with commendable fake stoicism. The task of letting me, a thirty three year old man seated on the examination bench in a treatment room at Bournemouth Hospital wearing only a pair of pants, know that my playing days were over.

I had been playing the injured card for some years, revelling in the 'getting old' jokes, while still competing against and beating much younger players. The injuries have got worse though, to the point where the joke isn't funny anymore and my right knee is not only very painful, but seriously affects my already affected game. In the back of my mind though, it was only ever going to be a trip to the doctors, some surgery, six weeks off, then playing on to age forty three, Sinjin Smith style.

The consultant had other ideas. He delivered his information with all the sensitivity of a man who was polishing off the days last appointment, leaving just enough time to play the back nine on the way home. He spoke of wear and tear, of basketball movements being responsible for my knees dilapidated state. I reminded him it was volleyball, he nodded, not breaking verbal stride and went on to his big finale. The consultant looked out of the treatment room window, as if to give dramatic effect but in reality looking like he was mentally testing the wind before his opening shot to the tenth, a three iron, lay up short of the bunkers, steady start. He turned back from the window and finally began to show his caring side. He delivered some one stop psychotherapy that seemed to be inspired by a black and white Department of Information cinema short. In a voice that had suddenly taken on a Mr Cholmondley-warner-esque tone, he said.

"Still, never mind you've had a good career...."

He was right, although he didn't actually know it. I am extremely lucky, I have had a really good career for one blessed with limited talent and physical ability. But that was what was making it all the more difficult to accept.

I started to protest, to question, but he held his hand up, smiled, told me the nurse would be in shortly and then, he left.

I sat in the room on my own for some minutes my thoughts racing and I don't know why, maybe a diversionary tactic, but I began some calculations about my playing career. I would imagine you may want to do something similar when you retire, it's very therapeutic. The mind boggles if you attempt some volleyball career calculations, a bit like looking up at a summer barbecue after your second lager and trying to imagine how big the universe is. The playing stats are easy enough, but my head starts to hurt when I try to work out miles travelled, sets played, money spent, games won and games lost. So I didn't bother. My playing career is not the longest by far and I hope the stats will keep mounting up with my continued interest in coaching, I wonder what statistics players like Stuart Fullerton, the legendary England middle blocker, could put together. Still playing solid division 1 volleyball at 42 years old.

I have now had a second opinion on my knee. It seems I can make one more beach season, but the cartilage is so worn it would be foolish not to hang up my knee pads and seek surgery to prolong the use of the knee for normal everyday purposes like standing-up, walking and kneeling for big finishes to show tunes.

I have just enjoyed an excellent season as player coach with Wessex in Division 1, shuffling my way through the games as a setter, my latest incarnation. When I moved on as player coach from Polonia at the end of the 1997-1998 season, I was ready to call it a day. I was really tired after driving to London three times a week from the New Forest, a two hour drive one way, to train and play. I'm glad I took the Wessex job. It gave me a chance to coach and play alongside some very talented and experienced players. It also meant I could continue working with Phil Allen, my assistant coach/team manager, who has been a fantastic and inspiring person to work with for the last two seasons. Making the Cup Final was a fitting reward for Phil, who has put so much into volleyball over a number of years.

The team lost 3-0 to Malory in the Final and finished runners-up to them in the league. I was satisfied along with several other long time players such as Anthony Roberts, Chris Eaton, Alex Bialokoz, Chris Whitbread and Clayton Lucas to make the Cup Final 2000 possibly my last official indoor game. It's hard to comprehend, to be faced with the proposition of re-inventing yourself after years of being known to volleyballers, friends and colleagues as a 'volleyball player'. However, with my first child now arrived, a couple of television contracts lined up and writing some books, I feel pretty well equipped to give it a go.

My incredibly lucky and successful season on the beach this summer, with Australian World Series player Tristan Boyd, has helped me become more relaxed about the prospect of stopping playing. You know it's going to happen one day, hopefully you have achieved many of your goals. You would also want to have some control over the final decision, but it's a really tough time in the life of any sports person. A lifetime away from the dreams, efforts and almost unbridled enthusiasm and dedication of the early playing years.

Student volleyball, confusion, beer, hard knocks, beer, great days, beer and Jordan 'Bloody' Hill........

It is difficult to describe to anyone who hasn't experienced student volleyball, the incredible nature of playing sport within the academic system. Time to train, time to play, very few costs other than beer and plenty of opportunities to progress. All of this taking place within an environment where everyone is at the same point in their lives, thinking and doing mostly the same things. You are surrounded by friends, both on your team and off, the intensity of student volleyball in my experience was never really repeated at club level. Only the beach has ever come close.

In 1983 I broke my thumb playing a one off volleyball game in a P.E lesson at Bexhill Sixth Form college in East Sussex. I clearly remember making the bold statement to my mother on the way back after yet another sport related hospital visit, that volleyball was definitely not the sport for me and that despite badly breaking a leg in a soccer match the previous year, I was determined to return to my first love, football.

I did return to football goalkeeping and signed a Southern league contract with Hastings United, just prior to taking up a place at West Sussex Institute of Higher Education (W.S.I.H.E pronounced 'Wishy'). A place which I was offered against all odds, following some truly awful A level results. A place which I was offered the night before the start of term and a place which brought me into contact with volleyball once again. The thought that I might not have gone to W.S.I.H.E worries me. I have received so much from volleyball and it has become such an integral part of my life that I cannot imagine not doing what I have done for the last fifteen years. I got my place at W.S.I.H.E when someone else dropped out of the course. I do not believe in fate, but I wonder how many other opportunities pass you by for one reason or another ?

I began college and played soccer and table tennis, I also dabbled in tennis, rugby, cricket and athletics. The defining volleyball moment in my College sports career came however, following a tragic soccer home game for the college. We had just lost 2-1 and in a style typical of an eighteen year old boy I became embroiled in a very nasty row with one of my own central defenders. He felt the goal which cost us the game was my fault. I cannot remember whether it was or it wasn't, but with a Southern League contract in my pocket I was not about to admit responsibility, I was a semi-pro. That's my way of saying it probably was my fault.

Admittedly I was receiving £15 per month (big money in 1985), but Hastings were not paying my travel back to games and they were calling me up less and less. If the truth be known I was a crap goalkeeper and I had reached the tremendously unnerving place where the player I thought I was did not match up with the spotty, six foot, skinny geek I saw on the video analysis at College. My confidence was shot following the my broken leg in 1983, I was never going to make it in the leagues and the sport I had played since my first toddling steps no longer seemed to hold the same allure of magical playing days gone by.

I trudged away from the pitch. A man drew alongside me, I recognised him as Nick Smith one of my Sports degree lecturers. Someone I had not had much to do with in my initial weeks at college, partly because I was a table tennis and soccer player (not his main sports) and partly because intelligent people scare me. His lectures, although brilliant and interesting, went straight over my head. It is a constant source of amusement to me that there seems to be an international call sign for Nick Smith lectures. Fifteen years on I still meet eighteen year old students lectured by Nick and I can say, "so, you're lectured by Nick Smith ?" When they confirm this fact, I simply wave my hand, palm down, over my head making a 'whooshing' sound. They always smile and nod their agreement. He just seemed to me to function on a way higher plane and sometimes it feels like he still does.

Nick said. "You don't look like you are enjoying yourself much. You should give volleyball a try, we train 8-10pm in the gym Tuesday's and Thursday's."

That was how it all started. I began to play and was one of the only freshers to stick-out Nick's legendary back to basics pre-season skills clinics which ran over the first few weeks of training. I stuck with it and so did one other student a huge lad, six foot ten he was. Unfortunately also completely 'unco', P.E student speak for uncoordinated, but great scare value when we turned up for games and paraded him past our opposition, watching their faces as he ducked under doorways.

By the end of the three weeks basic training I was hooked on the game, on the people in the team and on Nick's coaching. It was so new to listen to a coach who talked quietly, knowledgeably, who broke skills down and was patient. I had only ever encountered soccer managers who ran you into the ground, wouldn't know a drill if it bit them on the arse and shouted at you all the time.

"Golding what are you effing doing you effing stupid ponse. If you are going to catch the ball call for it you effing ginger haired git.....etc etc."

I am just paraphrasing of course, but the gist of soccer team talks seems to be that the players are all crap and they have to work harder and shout more, and a nice bit of spitting probably wouldn't go a miss.

Well in the West Sussex Institute gym, the atmosphere was totally alien to me and I really liked it. I found as time went on that I functioned well in the atmosphere of information and encouragement and revelled in being the junior on the team, basically unable to do any wrong.

The skills that I developed in that period are probably attributable to several factors. The first was Nick's coaching. Nick was an accomplished player in his own right, but more importantly an absolute scholar and genuine fan of the game.

He taught me the dig and the volley, I wanted like everyone to spike and block, but he insisted I work on dig and volley. It was boring in places and I really didn't understand why I had to work so hard on these skills, but six years later passing a German jump serve right where it should be passed, it all became blatantly obvious. Nick kept me focused, kept me working and kept my feet on the ground as I progressed quickly to a first team place.

Another factor was the team. A really great bunch of guys, all with the volleyball bug and all working hard to make the team successful. The team was special, I don't think that you ever recapture that feeling you have while playing for your first team. Having people around you that you respect and like, who do most of the work and take all the pressure.

The squad was formed largely from year two, three and four Physical Education students. The likes of Nick Robinson still playing volleyball in the Hampshire leagues and John Waters, Ashley Brown and Andy Wild are all teaching in the Hampshire area.

To be honest we were pretty hopeless, as Fergus Leslie our Captain and only real player once said to my Mother, "we (the team) couldn't hit a cow's arse with a banjo...."

Fergus was the driving force behind the team and a popular and successful choice as Captain. He was a short (5ft 8in) setter from Dundee, who doubled as very talented prop for the College rugby team. Fergus had real passion when he played and a fantastic sense of humour off the court. Every road trip on the College bus was made considerably more enjoyable by Fergus singing disgusting rugby songs or telling one of his elongated jokes. Jokes that involved additional storytelling, silly accents and Fergus helpless with laughter way before the punchline. Punchlines incidentally which were mostly less funny than the Celtic pre-amble that got the listeners to that point.

I suppose this is an appropriate time for an example of a Fergus gag, minus the accents and giggling of course.

A Fergus joke.........................

So, this bloke walks into a pub with his mate. They sit down and his mate gets the beers in. After a few sips of his pint, the bloke gets up and rubbing his stomach says 'must just pop to the loo.....I'm on the salts you see' Noises came from the toilet, the obvious fart like noises followed by shouts of 'hoi-hoopla'.

The bloke comes back from the loo and begins to drink. Then a few minutes later up he gets again. 'Just of to the loo', he explains. 'I'm on the salts you see.'

Same thing happens, some straining, some fart noises and lots of shouting.

Well, this happens another three times, each time accompanied by the explanation 'oooh! I'm on the salts!'

When the bloke gets up for a fourth time and heads for the loo his mate has had enough, so he decides to follow him. On arriving in the toilet the bloke is still shouting his head off in amidst some horrendous rip roaring postern blasts. His mate waits outside to confront him.

The bloke unlocks the door and out he comes and walks straight into to his mate who is standing there absolutely dumbstruck. He is gazing into the cubicle and it's horrible, shit absolutely everywhere, the walls, the floor, the ceiling and hardly any in the bowl. 'my god!' he shouts. 'what salts are you on?' "Somersaults!" says the bloke.

The gym itself also played an important role. Adverse circumstances often produce sporting legacies. Legend has it that Desmond Douglas learned his unique table tennis 'blocking' game because of the closeness of the lounge walls to the ends of his home table tennis table did not allow him to move more than a foot from the baseline. Bjorn Borg allegedly developed his ground strokes and patience because his village had no tennis court so he hit balls against his house wall every day for hours on end. Jose Loiola the Brazilian volleyball star developed his massive jump because he spent the first years of his life in callipers, like Forest Gump. When he finally got them off, the doctors gave him simple weights exercises to do on the sand and Jose did the exercises religiously, building up to hundreds of reps per day. After two years, he had developed a huge jump.

In the tiny confines of the W.S.I.H.E gym your skills had to develop quickly or the lack of space would make play impossible. The roof was low, very low. The beams that hung from it a metre from the net and into court at positions two and four either side of the net, were even lower. Dig too high you hit a beam, set too far off the net you hit a beam. We hit the beams a lot, but our visiting opponents hit them more. We insisted on no 'let' and gave a fault everytime a beam was hit, it made some opponents extremely angry.

The gym was and still is an enigma. It is a wooden throw back to a bygone age of military style gymnastics, there was barely room for a court let alone posts for a net. The previous year Nick had joined the college staff and set up the volleyball club, stringing a net across the width of the gym. The following year the net was made permanent by attaching a yacht winch to one wall and cleats to the opposite wall.

Putting the net up was a peculiar skill. Winding the rope on and then tensioning it with the winch, accompanied by lots of creaking noises as the net tension increased. If you had set it up wrong initially, the whole thing could go twang, rope snaking off the winch like line off of a fishing reel when you've hooked the big one.

At the far end of the gym was the spectator balcony, the 'balcony' became a symbol of manhood, a rite of passage. It was only ten or so feet off of the ground behind one of the baselines, but it became a pilgrimage, a holy grail for male W.S.I.H.E players. To bounce the ball off of the floor from a spike and up into the balcony was the stuff of legend and the male of the species, were he to achieve this feat, would take on a certain world-ly-wise aura. 'Yes young lady, I am familiar with the ways of the balcony'.

Hitting the ball up into the balcony was achieved only twice by the team in my first season. Both times it was by our shortest player and setter, Fergus. Fergus, who had been taught to play volleyball by Scottish legend John Scringeour, was our only real player. He had good skills, a nice pair of hands and because of years of cycling time trials the biggest set of quads I have ever seen on a volleyball player. This particular anatomical feature enabled Fergus to absolutely launch himself into the air, he had a massive jump and could dunk a basketball at playtime with the big boys.

At the time, we of little volleyball knowledge, thought our Captain's ability to put the ball in the balcony to be a huge demonstration of power.

How things change as we grow and learn from experiences. I have, in my time, roofed the ball in that small W.S.I.H.E gym. At the other end of the spectrum in the World Student games I watched in awe as screaming Germans roofed ball after ball in the warm-up at Ponds Forge, something no longer achievable with the new ball pressures. But for us, in 1985, the W.S.I.H.E balcony was Everest.

In contrast to the balcony hit was the more frequently achieved membership of the 'back wall club'. Entry to this, 'not very exclusive club', was gained simply by hitting a ball, still rising as it passed over the baseline straight into the wall (no bounce remember) which was but a few feet from the end of the court. Shots like this were always greeted with howls of derision and the usual calls 'lost in space' etc.

Within weeks of beginning my volleyball odessy I had given up football, pretty much for good.

My volleyball progressed well and I began to get the hang of it, after a fashion. Competitive opportunities at College however where largely coming from table tennis. It's a strange sport, table tennis. I was only into it because my girlfriend at the time played the game. I was not particularly good, but good enough to play for the College in the West Sussex League (yes, there is such a thing).

Table tennis diplomacy, smelly uncles and sanctions...

It is a generally acknowledged phenomena, familiar I would imagine to most of you, that local leagues in any sport hate students. The Sussex volleyball league hated us, I never knew why. We were well organised, well coached and one of our senior players helped to run the league. The table tennis league though, showed another level of student hatred altogether.

I was secretary of the Table Tennis team and had to organise two players alongside me for each match. The two players who formed the team with me were a constant source of entertainment and frustration. I was serious about the game and still new to the sport, they had played for years, they were bored and they definitely were not....serious that is.

Week in week out though, in dingy village halls, playing against fifty year old stalwarts of the local sporting community, Matt Easdown and David Spicer completed my College line up.

I would try to be nice, respectful and mature to opponents during the games. I was keen to create a good impression with the local clubs, all highly suspicious of student teams and/or anyone under sixty. Matt and Dave tended to see the evening as an opportunity to embarrass me and generally have a good laugh however.

Within weeks their student high spirits were clashing head on with local sports community stoicism. They never did anything really bad or hideously disrespectful. They simply larked about, got the giggles on occasion and worst of all, they won most of their games. The consequence was that we were public enemy number one and threatening the top teams and the very puritan fabric of the West Sussex Table Tennis League.

Letters began to flood in from 'concerned' players. Players that were of course only too happy to see the students enter the league, but nevertheless worried that we might not be completely serious about the whole thing. Serious about it ? You didn't have to be Inspector Morse to figure out that when three teenage lads get uncontrollable giggles because one of their number has introduced himself as 'Spicker' instead of 'Spicer' that the very fabric of the league was not foremost in their minds.

So we played on and the complaints continued. The lighting in our sports hall was substandard, our table was not regulation, our blackout curtains on the windows were not properly drawn. All unbelievable stuff and all quite wrong. The real problem was us, young lads having a laugh and winning.

It all came down to the two teams sharing top place in the league with us, constantly complaining about us. I was called to a disciplinary hearing after a team in Bognor had behaved pathetically when we beat them at our place. Their Captain demanded the match was voided because of our lighting and Matt stepped in to the diplomatic breech and told him to 'piss off!'

Because of Matt's response to what was preposterous behaviour from our opponents, we were docked points and ordered to replay the match at Bognor. The evening of the match Matt turned up in the College minibus to drive us to the game. It was overkill to have three players in the bus, but we asked no questions and set off.

When we arrived at the venue we headed into the hall, while Matt who said he had something to do in town drove off in the bus. I was first into the hall and the reception was frosty to say the least. It was not shaping up to be a pleasant game. Half way through the warm up Matt walked in and following him were three incredibly smelly old tramps. Each tramp was holding a brand new two litre bottle of triple strength lager, purchased for them by their new best friend, Matt.

"What the hell do you think you're doing ?" asked the Bognor Captain.

"My Uncles have come to watch me play." replied Matt, deadpan.

The Captain scowled at him, but surprisingly offered no further challenge, students were after all 'the spawn of the devil' and therefore maybe these three hideous apparitions were actual relatives. We proceeded to thrash our opponents. Our fan club got more and more drunk and began to shout at each winning shot. We milked it and did high fives with them, while they continued to drink.

By the last game, Matt versus the Bognor Captain, it was near riot. One of the tramps kept shouting that he was going to burn the hut down. Another sat and smiled angelically looking toward the ceiling while urine bubbled through his trousers like a grotesque fountain. The uncles stunt wasn't a pleasant thing to do, but it was a master stroke in sporting revenge.

I was summoned by the league once again for disciplinary action. I stuck to the 'uncles' story and we were granted one more chance. This time we were due to play Midhurst, now top of the league and fielding three of the most pompous, dishonest and blatantly anti-student players in the league.

We jumped into a taxi for the away game. Matt and Dave's idea, so that after the game we could enjoy an end of season drink together. I knew it was not going to go well when we arrived and Dave ordered three pints for each of us. We sat in the bar and got absolutely mullered. Dave and Matt decided that we were going to be pro-players that night.

The latest pro-table tennis craze was to apply bicycle puncture repair glue to the bat and the underside of the sponge rubber. The fumes from the glue would fill the cells in the rubber and increase the speed of the bat to ridiculous proportions. Accompanying this speed and spin was a characteristic and very loud 'Tak!' noise which echoed around the hall.

We headed down to the hall for the game and staggered in reeking of beer and teetering right on the edge of an uncontrollable laughter precipice. Dave and Matt drank five pints each, I got to four and was in serious bother with my co-ordination. Our hosts were not amused, but saw their opportunity to beat the students and take the league title.

I was first up and because we were late down to the hall we were denied our warm-up. So as the first serve came towards me in this historic game, my bat stinking of bike glue, I was overcome by pro-table tennis euphoria. I took an almighty swing at the ball and absolutely creamed it. 'Tak!' boomed around the hall and the ball shot back to the server at lightening speed. He had no chance to move and the ball hit him straight in the toilet region. Table tennis balls are light and seemingly harmless, but at speed they can really sting.

The Midhurst Captain slumped forward over the table clutching at his crown jewels and experiencing the kind of pain that is both impossible to describe by a man and surely difficult to imagine by women who have not experienced child birth. Matt and Dave, pissed and carefree began to laugh openly. Dave fell sideways off his chair absolutely screaming with laughter. I was trying to keep mine under control and rushed to the aid of my stricken opponent. He turned his face to meet my concerned gaze. "You bloody little shit!" he shouted. "You did that on purpose." The situation calmed and we played on. I was hopeless and lost all three of my games. Matt and Dave came alive and soundly stuffed Midhurst out of sight amid gales of laughter. Easily one of the best evenings of sport I have ever been involved in.

Naturally we were suspended from the league and the title awarded to Midhurst by default. A small price to pay.

My first volleyball game. great keeper, bad defender....

Trying to compete in the volleyball league was a completely different challenge. My first game is still vivid in my memory. A pre-season friendly had been arranged by Nick with the mighty Havant Pumas, Div.3 South N.V.L. Like a primary school kid in a school football match I was completely clueless about the team we were playing and their standard of play. All I knew was I wanted to play volleyball.

I had been on the team a month, everything was still a blur. Remember when you first played and rotations were like Vulcan mind transfers. That was how I viewed this game. Like many cognitive learners (beginners, I put that psychology stuff in to impress my students) I was still counting out loud when I ran in to spike. I had been taught to shout 'switch' to myself to remind me to do just that after our service and was playing middle blocker so there were two experienced players either side of me to stop me disappearing past the aerial and out of the door on over enthusiastic blocks.

I was benched for almost the entire game and the pace from the sidelines looked incredible. It didn't matter though, I was desperate to get on court. It was 12 - 5 to Havant in the third set, they were two sets to nil, when I was given the nod. Safe in the knowledge that we had lost it was deemed appropriate to bring on the new kid. I probably thought I was going to turn it around.

I was brought on in back court, position six. My agility from goalkeeping had transferred well to volleyball defence. We served and I set up, no joking I was so stoked I could have pissed myself with exitement. I was actually on court and playing. That was as good as it got though. With so much information in my head and my arousal levels sky high my chances of remembering, let alone executing a recognisable volleyball skill, were zilch.

25

It all happened in my first point on court, the Havant players ran a cross-over play on the net. I didn't know it was a cross-over at the time, that had to be explained later. All I knew was that for some bizarre reason one Havant player had jumped along with all three of my blockers. The Havant player had landed and so had my blockers and emerging over their heads and the net band, like a bird of prey from behind a motorway hedgerow, was a second Havant player. I watched from my back court position as the play unfolded. A shoot out, just me and him.

He hit the ball hard and I went diving quickly and full length to my right, catching the ball with both hands and hanging on to it as I hit the deck. Yes! I thought, not only I had stopped it from going into the goal, but I had held on to it as well.

With that single ridiculous, but nevertheless skilful action, I had earned my place in the team's psyche. The story still gets recounted when I meet with them at various tournaments and teaching conferences.

The season continued on. I got better as a player, I caught the ball less in defence and I got more court time. By April of the following year I was a starting six middle blocker and so ready for the British Colleges Finals in York that I would have gladly quit college and moved to that city just so I wouldn't miss a single point.

York 1986, McKenzie, Banks and all that jazz...........

Nick called a training camp, like a proper team would do. It was one of the best weeks I have ever had in volleyball.

The team arrived in Chichester, with sleeping bags and kit. We slept on Nick and Carole's (Nick's wife) lounge floor for three days prior to leaving for York and completed the team bonding process. We trained everyday, ate, drank and watched Police Academy videos. We talked endlessly about the tournament and began writing our opening call. It was fashionable back then to produce some reasonably lengthy shouts. In short, the whole week was volleyball heaven.

It was a very innocent volleyball age, pre-Ralph Hippolyte. It was a time when a 'mindset' meant you had just headed the ball, when a 'free ball' was something you won at a tournament raffle and when the only thing that a second movement ever blocked was 'Portaloo' at a summer tournament.

The W.S.I.H.E team played in the Sussex league and competed fairly well. One or two of us could even spike the ball over the net, downhill with the wind behind us that is.

In March 1986 we beat some absolutely dire opposition to qualify for the British Colleges finals for the first time in W.S.I.H.E history. According to us we were a crack squad of deadly volleyball assassins. In truth the only people we were ever going to kill would be the ones that breathed in the rancid air we had generated on the team minibus. This whole sad misunderstanding about our supposed talents had come about because coach Smith had failed to point out that our opponents in the qualifying tournament were about as useful as the England back four at a European Soccer Finals.

It was difficult to say what we thought we could assassinate with six rock hard volleyballs, two midget setters and an assortment of failed rugby, soccer and tennis players. Our skills were solid, but our hitting was wild and erratic. To be honest remaining inside the court area when playing against us was probably the safest option because, like a cross-eyed hammer thrower, we certainly kept the crowd on their toes.

We arrived in York blissfully ignorant of what real volleyball was. Cocooned in local league euphoria and with the odd shandy inside us, we were convinced, to a man, that we were 'the' team. We had no idea what an international player was or for that matter what made them better than us. Nick decided to let us enjoy our last night out of hospital in blissful ignorance, never once mentioning the teams we were about to face.

I spent a hideous first night in York. My room mate, the large uncoordinated bloke, tended to get morose after a few pints and for two hours back at the room he sobbed uncontrollably and made some pretty grim statements about his life and where it was going. He then decided to stagger, wailing incoherently, around the room, before collapsing on the floor and going to sleep. Not my idea of a good nights rest.

The morning of the tournament came and I was up at 5.00am feeling sick as a dog, with nerves about the impending event. We were all reduced to almost complete silence at the breakfast table. Finally departure time arrived and we filed onto the bus to drive up to the sports centre. We entered the hall in our shirts and ties looking as mean as we could, you know the routine. During one particularly face wrenching bout of looking 'hard' my Grandparents, who had come to watch me play, walked in. Ignoring my volleyball assassin's sneer, my Grandma took my face in her hands, kissed my cheek and handed me some sandwiches. Luckily for me only ninety-nine percent of the tournament participants witnessed the incident.

I had just worked tirelessly with my team mates to give the impression that I only ate rusty nails, broken glass and small babies. My Nan handed me some white bread cheese and Marmite sandwiches with the crusts cut off.

Still high on our ridiculous and as yet unchallenged confidence, we

27

changed in good spirits for our first game against Jordan Hill College. Our coach, Nick, told us that they were a Scottish P.E institution. Surely they wouldn't be very good, oh well! we all live and learn.

The general warm up finished and the referee blew for hitting through four. Not a major incident in world volleyball I grant you, but for me and the team a seminal moment in our volleyball careers. When the whistle blew it was still all about us and what we were going to do in this momentous warm-up. I was the acknowledged lead gunner by virtue of the fact that on a good day my spikes went over the net and into court most consistently. It was, after much preparation, my chance to deliver a patented thump-mungous, topspintastic spike on the unsuspecting Jordan Hill team and the soon to be infatuated crowd. Their screams were already ringing in my ears.

My early spikes really had to be seen to be fully believed. They started with a gradual rocking back and fourth, similar to a top class long jumper achieving a full psyche-up and visualising the successful jump. For me though it was a chance to do all my counting, one two and left right in my head, pre-spike. As we improve in the art of hitting we develop a grooved and generally economical technique. Just think back though, to what it used to be like. Not only was each spike attempt an individual entity, but they could mostly be described as a mammoth frenzy of arms and legs, from which on occasion a ball would emerge.

My clear instructions had been to approach from only as far away as the three metre line, to minimise the potential for hilarious disaster. I of course assumed that I had been told this to protect the innocent people that might get hurt if I were to take a full run up. Here in York it seemed to be an appropriate arena to unleash 'the big one'. The mother of all spikes, the 'pay load'. With this in mind and with Jordan Hill still casually removing track-suits, the stage was all mine.

Stunned spectators watched as I retreated to a new take off position, about a metre in from the baseline. I heaved a feed into Fergus the setter which had so much spin and height on it that by the time it got to his hands sparks flew off of his finger tips and set light to the cuffs of his nylon W.S.I.H.E volleyball shirt. Using the fingers of steel technique he managed a great set which floated invitingly above the net tape. A net tape which incidentally was some considerable distance away from me. My time had come.

I started my stuttering, swerving run up, attempting to co-ordinate my skinny little legs to deliver me to an approximate take off spot. I had now reached optimum launch speed, which basically equated to maximum velocity forward converted into minimum height upwards, but it felt good.

I left the floor with a triumphant whoop (believe me this is painful to recount), feeling a whoop would impress any female spectators and scare the bejesus out of the Jordan Hill players. In reality I did nothing more than throw myself into the air, with my legs apart in an almost pornographic star jump. I twitched out my right arm like an octogenarian darts player and just about made contact with the ball. It travelled toward the net slowly enough for all around me to freeze and chart it's progress. The ball caught the net tape and dropped harmlessly in to court on the other side, bouncing lamely and coming to rest just over the three metre line.

No one could have been impressed with the shot, but in our eighteen by nine metre sprung wood kingdom that was forever the W.S.I.H.E gym, the spike was an absolute peach. Naturally I turned to receive the plaudits of my team, who were ecstatic at my incredible display of power. It seemed to us that Jordan Hill had only one option, to surrender.

Then a massive noise rent the air, very close to where I was standing. My head snapped forward and I hunched my shoulders. The sort of reaction one produces almost involuntarily when a banger goes off within close range or someone shouts 'lookout!'

'KABOOM!' the noise echoed around the hall and as I recovered my composure I noticed a volleyball soaring upwards towards the roof of the building, peaking, then beginning it's long decent back to the sports hall floor. Ian McKenzie, Scottish senior international, a six foot four bull of a man, had done the deed. He landed stepped under the net and treated me to his version of looking hard. To this day I swear he actually does eat rusty nails, broken glass and small babies.

The W.S.I.H.E team froze. Nobody had told us that there were people who could do that to a volleyball. It was obscene, it was magic and it was going to be coming directly towards our innocent childlike faces following the warm-up. Some players approached Nick on the sideline clutching groins and suggesting it would be an opportunity to give the bench a run out.

The more foolhardy among us re-grouped in mid court and looked intently through the net at the next Jordan Hill player in the team. We heaved a collective sigh of relief, it was only a small ginger haired lad, about five foot ten. Thank god for that, they were a one man team.

The small ginger haired boy coasted into the net and jumped, boy did he jump. 'KABOOM!' went the ball and his bigger team mate's shot was repeated with interest. His name was Brian Banks, Scottish international number two. For those of you who never saw Brian Banks in action, his playing style and ability could have made him Jurek Jankowski's twin brother, but with curly hair.

Banks landed and smiled straight at us, a kind of you may take our

29

kneepads, but you will never take our freedom smile. We were now officially scared and nothing else could have made us feel worse. Until our Captain, Fergus, not one for using rose tinted spectacles said in a chilling voice "Bastard!"

"Yeh, Bastard!" I agreed.

"No, look." Said Fergus. "He's still got his bloody flip flops on!"

This was too much for the remaining players. One of the middle hitters fainted and our bench setter, Ashley Brown, was lead away in tears. Tears of laughter I suspect as he realised he was not going to have to be on court.

The warm-up continued in a similar vein. Twelve embarrassed W.S.I.H.E players wafting increasingly pathetic hits across the net, while Ian McKenzie repeatedly leathered one ball after another on to the floor with all the finesse of a building site pile driver. Brian Banks on the other hand flew this way and that, holding various poses for the press before nailing the ball.

The whistle blew and some of the W.S.I.H.E players rushed over to the hitting area to check the court for scorch marks. Some just retired to the toilets to check for skidmarks.

Then suddenly we remembered, we still had one last chance to knock the Jordan Hill machine from it's well oiled runners, our call. Remember I said that long shouts at the beginning of games had become quite the thing ? Well, on the minibus journey up we had devised a belter. A real humdinger, a fearsome musical call guaranteed to strike terror in to the hearts of any opponent. In reality it was the longest and most embarrassing pre-match call ever heard. It took nearly a minute to get through and went something like, if not exactly like, this...............

"On the south coast down at Chichester, where the yanks have never been,
There's a bunch of W.S.I.H.E students, who make up the volleyball team,
Wherever we may go and wherever we have been,
You will always hear us sing this song,
we are the W.S.I.H.E volleyball team...."

(and there is more...with the actions, naturally)

"Swing a chicken in the air,
Stick a deck chair up your nose,
Fly a jumbo jet and then bury all your clothes,
Get your willy's out and give us a shout,
We are the W.S.I.H.E volleyball team,
Just saaaaaaaayyyyyyyy......yes!"

I know it is unbelievable, but we really did sing it.

We hoped to demoralise the Jordan Hill players. Why on earth a load of pimply students cavorting backwards and forwards in Dunlop Greenflash trainers singing the most contrived lyrics since Marillion's last hit, should ever scare another team is now, with the benefit of hindsight, quite beyond me. But, when you're up to your eyeballs in it, I suppose you will try anything.

Nick stood patiently by on the sidelines. I occasionally like to remind him of that call, now buried fifteen years back in his memories, but still more than capable of getting him to involuntarily pull his lips way back behind his gum line and draw a sharp intake of breath in vivid remembrance.

The crowd was now firmly on our side, having clearly spotted the underdogs they gave us a sympathetic cheer. Spurred on by this nugget of encouragement we struck a group pose like some homies in a rap video, but probably looking more like homos in a village people video. Then the Jordan Hill call cut through the pre-game atmosphere like a very big axe. 'Jordaaaaan Hill!" and that was it. Simple, effective and just a little bit vicious.

"What shall we do?" said the team. Captain Fergus had the Monty Python answer. "Run away!" he shouted.

We played like nutters and held it together for fifteen minutes. We actually competed against a team which could field two international and four national league players. I even got a roof block on McKenzie to make it five points all. With each play we grew in confidence and began to feel that we had every right to be on court. Then it all went pear shaped and in one split second we were reminded of who we had stepped on to court with.

The ball was set wide to McKenzie and my opposite middle blocker, Paul Andrews, had jumped with their quick middle. This left a one on one with McKenzie and Fergus, who valiantly formed his block as far away from McKenzie as he could get. It was time to pull off another defensive play in the back court. Mckenzie hit the ball. The last time a ball had come at me this quick it was struck by Peter Heritage a former Hastings United striker who was sold on to Gillingham. On that occasion I was knocked of my feet and into the goal. This time around it was Ian McKenzie who had absolutely mashed it and I was frozen where I stood. The only defensive movement I made was to shut my mouth and eyes.

SMACK! the ball hit me square in the face. The sound resonated around my skull and I went down like a sack of spuds. My first Mikasa facial tat-

31

too. The ball left my forehead and hit the ceiling, I simply left the court. The team struggled on but, Jordan Hill had found their rhythm and it was all over in twenty minutes. Yeh! all over my face.

We left the sports hall that evening having lost all three of our games. But, we were no longer volleyball virgins.

That night we visited the Spread Eagle public house in York. An appropriate epitaph to the events of the day. We drank and talked for hours. It emerged that Fergus had in fact spoken with Brian Banks in the changing rooms after the game. Folklore has it that Mr Banks told Fergus that we had played well. That was it then, for the rest of that season Banks and McKenzie were names we banded about whenever we made a big shot. Just like when you used to play soccer in the garden and pretend to be your hero. For me at World Cup time, as a goalkeeper, I was only ever Dino Zoff or Sepp Meyer. I'm showing my age now.

The other phenomenon that came out of the tournament was one that we see across the board in sports, copying the stars fashions. Turning collars up, socks pulled over the knee and lycra. McKenzie and Banks both wore only one kneepad, we thought that was so cool. For the remainder of the season we all only wore one kneepad, our form of hero worship, half crippling ourselves every time we dived.

I met Brian Banks at a Services tournament in 1996, me playing for GB Civil Service and Brian playing for GB Fire Service. I spoke to Brian about the York tournament over a beer and what he said to me confirmed his star status at the time.

"Sorry mate, I don't remember any of that!" he laughed.

Crewe and Alsager, 1987.
A second bite at the cherry....

Over my three years at college the team changed. The two constants were myself and Fergus. Our first excursion to the British Colleges Final had left us with a very real desire to win Gold, before our student days were over.

In December 1986, Nick Smith left W.S.I.H.E to return to his former college Crewe and Alsager, now Manchester Metropolitan University. We were devastated at his departure, but had been left in the capable hands of Simon Coleman, a product of Nick's Crewe and Alsager Gold medal winning team of 1983. The team held great respect for Simon, not only because of his

32

coaching qualities, but because he was a current first division player with newly promoted Portsmouth Heatseal. Simon also used to put the ball in the balcony on a regular basis, consequently he found it relatively easy to become the chief of our little tribe.

As a coach Simon was maybe more adventurous than Nick and was good for the team. We continued to develop. The 1987 British Colleges was hosted at Crewe and Alsager by Nick Smith. Time was running out for Fergus and myself, if we failed this year we only had one more shot at the Gold.

We were out of luck. The rules concerning which colleges could qualify had changed and Scotland were able to enter two colleges. The sixteenth British Colleges Volleyball Finals was attended by Jordan Hill (of course) who had an even better team supporting Brian Banks and Ian McKenzie with Donny McLeod, David Brodie and Danny Clarke. Without a shadow of doubt from game one on Saturday it was clear to all of us that their only real opponents would be Strathclyde College, captained by Iain Cook (Cookie, Scottish international), with Iain Grubb (Great Britain captain) and James Orr (Scottish senior international). It was a bloody fix! We crashed and burned.

Crewe and Alsager, 1988.
The last chance saloon.........

The 1988 finals were mine and Fergus's last chance for the gold. The team we took to that years Finals were still a mix and match outfit, but overall we were stronger. Fergus and myself had played a whole season in NVL division three south with Sussex Nomads and that had given us confidence and developed our skills. We were supported by new players like Steve Richards (former Purbrook Park player), Rob Harley, Simon Northcott, Jim Barker (Milton Keynes NVL), George Zorzi and Chris Harty.

Jordan Hill now bereft of it's key players failed to qualify and Strathclyde were no longer an eligible college. The door of opportunity was slightly open. Our main competitors were Moray House containing Scottish Juniors Alex Gunn and Steve Milne and Liverpool, a one man team of Phil Newton, the England and Great Britain senior international and one of the most talented players this country has ever produced.

Preparations went well, until I tried to get off the bus on arrival at Alsager. My back had gone into spasm and I really couldn't move, I couldn't even stand up straight.

The team were very supportive and touchingly disappointed. We had no replacement middle blocker. Fergus was upset at my injury to say the least. Under these unfortunate circumstances we were left with no option, but to head off for the legendary Crewe and Alsager student union bar and go drinking.

The Alsager bar was huge. It was great because it was friendly, there was always a buzz and at the end of the evening the disco finished the night with 'Tiger Feet' by Mud, a brilliant opportunity for some vintage crap dancing.

We got very pissed and the gold medal no longer seemed as precious as we had previously assumed. The evening wore on and as was the tradition in the Alsager campus bar, the pool tables were stacked on top of each other (all three of them) for a spot of table diving.

I was still doubled up, although the beer was helping ease the pain. Fergus insisted that I came up with the team to catch some table divers. I linked arms with Fergus and a W.S.I.H.E team member, Rob Harley the team poseur and all-round star bloke, dived from his lofty perch. He descended towards us and the catchers alongside Fergus and myself disappeared, for a laugh. Fergus and I caught Rob between us and my back made a really loud crack and clunk noise. I anticipated agony, but the relief was immediate. I could stand up and it felt great. The game was now well and truly back on.

We cruised to Final, which was a strange affair. I had just coached the women's team to a 3 - 2 loss to Crewe and Alsager, coached by Nick. It was an extremely long and stressful game, two hours and forty five minutes. The W.S.I.H.E team had done incredibly well against their lofty opponents who started several experienced players including Jo Powell the former Welsh international and Sale player.

By the time the men came on court to play I was out of it, over psyched after the women's game. The length of the women's game however, had done us a favour that we were completely unaware of until the game was in full swing.

We were playing against Liverpool Institute, a team carried by the mighty Phil Newton. He was an incredible player over the years and was awesome in the finals hitting warm-up.

First point went well, I roofed Phil and the team went berserk. That was the last he let us see of the ball in set one and we went down 15-6. Once again Fergus, myself and the team were watching the gold medal drift away.

The two teams came out for the second set and after closer inspection by us we realised Phil Newton was not on court. We looked around for him and he was not on the bench either. Hope began to return and was turned into near hysterical joy when the opposition captain, Neil Smith, admitted to Fergus that Phil had stayed as long as he could, but had rushed off to a national league game for Liverpool.

W.S.I.H.E got things under control and we sailed through to a three one win and gold, at last. It was a special moment after so many great times attending the championships. We celebrated properly, jumping on each other and cracking bottles of champagne in the changing rooms.

The legendary student 'Triangulars'...............

When I had left W.S.I.H.E I was still able to compete as a student in representative squads. Out of the blue Endsleigh Insurance picked up the student sponsorship tab and re-launched the triangular challenge. The triangular events were incredible student gatherings over the Easter week. The Polytechnics, Universities and Colleges would turn out teams in a multitude of different sports volleyball, soccer, netball, hockey, badminton, swimming, basketball and on.

The students from every sport for each educational institution would be hosted at one central venue, it was massive and must have cost a fortune. Every player received free kit and goody bag, all courtesy of the sponsor. An absolutely fantastic time was had by all.

In 1989 I represented the Colleges team in my year out. The tournament was hosted at Loughborough University and it was awesome.

We actually played very badly as the college team and we were hopelessly outclassed by the other teams. My memories of the tournament were the final night ceremony and party, which I will come to in a moment, and the emergence again of a worrying part of my game.

I had always been hot headed, something coaches had dealt with well. My temper however was starting get the better of me in certain situations, especially situations where I was having to take a bigger share of responsibility than I was normally used to.

I see this phenomena now with young players that I coach gradually taking on more pressure for their team and responding sometimes with truculence and anger to the situation.

On the last day in Loughborough, with nothing on the line and playing our last match against the Polytechnic team, I received a red card. It is the only time it has happened to me. It could have happened more but for the intelligence and skill of some coaches and referees around me.

I had got into a very negative mood about the last game we were playing and losing. I was behaving like a spoilt kid and being nasty to team mates. I challenged the referee unfairly on several occasions about his decisions and he had just about put up with as much as he could take. My next piece of abuse was met with a yellow card. He brandished the yellow card and I strolled slowly over to him and looked intently at the piece of card he was holding up. Then with all the dignity and self control I could muster I said in a loud voice, "what's that then, your bus pass ?". That was it, red card.

It was stupid in the context of the game. A good story in hindsight though and one of those said what you wanted to say just at the right time moments, that happen so rarely. The usual format being to think about what you would have liked to have said hours later.

My other memory of the Loughborough Triangular tournament was the closing ceremony. The wine with the meal was supplied free, a bold move. We felt duty bound to drink it and by the end of the presentations we were slaughtered. It was a great evening of carefree dancing and singing. The mayor who was making the presentations, did so with a couple of students snogging furiously against the wall, directly behind him.

I knew things were going a little too well when I sidled up to group of girls and tried to impress them by dancing to 'Jump' by Van Halen. When the chorus came around I jumped as high as I could and next thing I knew I was on the floor. I wonder if the girls were in fact impressed ?

I was picked up by my equally unstable team mates. The evening continued at length until I decided I had to go to the toilet. My sense of direction is poor when I am sober, when I am drunk it is dreadful. After what seemed like an age of walking round the student union I ended up outside and positioned myself in front of a large bush to begin weeing. The effort of passing water was too much and as I widdled I remember this feeling of falling forwards, which was highly appropriate, because I was falling forwards. I fell into the bush and lay there unable to stop weeing or to get up, giggling uncontrollably.

Luckily for me, some college basketball players picked me up and handed me back my pint glass. They pointed me in the direction of my room and I staggered off into the night. On coming to the curb outside my halls of residence I had a small accident and dropped my pint glass it smashed on the road, something that will become relevant later.

I got into my room, somehow, and attempted to apply my tried and trusted method for checking whether I was really pissed and if I would therefore be ill the next day. I do not know why we should want to assess our sobriety, especially when in possession of irrefutable evidence which suggests we are absolutely hammered. I think most of you have some sort of 'am I pissed assessment system.' Mine involves finding my current book, if I can read some of the paragraphs then I am probably going to be O.K! Read my book ? I could not even bloody well find my book. I searched for ages and eventually located the publication. I got into bed and opened the book, the lines all melted into one blob and I found it impossible to make out a single word. My hypothesis was confirmed I was indeed pissed.

There is a moral to the story however, and you will be delighted to know that I was very ill the next morning. The only redeeming feature was that while on a hang-over ridden 7.00am stumble round the campus I was sick on the Mathematics department doorstep. I hate maths.

On returning to head off home with my lift I came across a team mate with his car full of extremely ill players. They were parked outside my halls and he was sat by the car looking very upset. This is where I submit my own confession to the Simon Mayo show. The reason their car was stopped was because they had a puncture. The car was a hire car and the spare was flat and they were waiting for the AA to show up. The puncture had evidently been caused by a "bloody broken pint glass, left in the road." Whoops!

I was in no fit state to admit my part in their downfall and slunk back to my room to fetch my bags and leave. The horrendous journey home was spent under a blanket, stopping to vomit every twenty minutes. On arrival at my house I used the time honoured "must have eaten something last night, few other people were also ill etc etc" and headed off to bed.

Leaving student volleyball was the first real watershed in my playing career. It is good to move on, but without doubt I will always look back on my student volleyball years with great affection.

38

Chapter 2
The Road to Sheffield

The World Student Games, Sao Paulo 1989.
My first attempt.....................

It was 7.30am on a cold, dark November morning 1988 and I was sat in my parents lounge in Hampshire staring at a small non-descript brown envelope, which I held in my hand. The envelope had arrived at 7.00am but, as with any envelope bearing vital news, I was finding it really hard to open. After all, the longer the envelope remained shut and it's contents unread, the longer I remained in the World Student Games squad bound for Sao Paulo in Brazil.

This tremendously lonely moment was the culmination of a procedure that had begun many months earlier when myself and Fergus had filled out application forms for the GB student trials, while sitting in the W.S.I.H.E dinning hall. Then hot footed it to the post box on campus.

I was now deliberately lingering over discovering whether I was in or out. I had already considered the 'in' part, in fact it had dominated my thoughts over recent months. It was the 'out' scenario that was troubling me. If I was out it was going to feel like losing a match, but probably much worse. The sharp sting, that subsides eventually to a dull ache, of knowing that at that particular moment you just weren't good enough, you had lost and someone else had won. That feeling is almost certainly one of the key elements in playing sport.

In my experience, the winners, the people who succeed most often are the players who manage to exclude from their thoughts that feeling of absolute desolation at a loss while actually competing. I think that is why they feel the loss all the more acutely. Because when it does actually happen, it had been so far from the conscious thought, that on the final whistle it hits them like a train. It comes as a shock, a surprise. Those players hate it, but the best ones learn from it and use that desolate feeling to fuel their future efforts.

I already had an inkling of what the envelope contained, because the previous months trials had held several clues.

In late Summer of 1988 I was invited to a trial at Birmingham University. I was now at Capital City playing division 1 NVL which gave me some confidence, but also meant I now knew a number of the players attending the trial and I knew they were good. Alex Bialokoz, Phil Davies,

Phil Bone, Paul Conlon and Iain Grubb to name but a few.

The trials were like nothing I had ever experienced before. Not only did the coaches, Keith Nicholls and John Lyle, want to see you play, but they also wanted to directly measure what all forty two players could do. I lined up with all the other players to have my height, weight, sprint time, standing jump and broad jump measured at the start of the trial.

I had completed a couple of tests, damaging my ankle in the broad jump, and was now in the queue for the standing jump. I would be O.K, I thought. In my own sports hall gym I could comfortably touch the basketball ring from a standing jump. So my turn came and I moved into position, with chalk on my finger tips ready to mark my effort on the wall. I had been in other queue's recording other statistics so I had not paid any attention to the standing jump area which probably added to the shock as I realised my task.

I looked up to view what I felt would be my touching zone, it was pretty clean, almost no chalk dust. Optimistically I dropped my stare to just below 'my' zone, it was still clean except for one set of finger prints, which I suspect were Paul Conlon's (the Stoke City setter). My only other option was to look up, and up. There, about a foot above 'my' zone was a clutch of prints that looked like someone making a grab for a penthouse suite balcony and only just missing. A further foot up from those prints was a set all on their own. The owner had clearly grabbed the balcony, with both hands and was currently reclining on the Penthouse chaise long sipping an ice cold beer.

The heighest set of finger prints belonged to Alex Bialokoz, two metre tall Great Britain and England player. Alex was stood the other side of the coach and had just jumped, which is why the coach was still dribbling and smiling like a lovesick teenager. I was going to jump straight after Alex and my neck was already stiffening from looking up at his mark.

If I had just been about to be fingerprinted for the murder of a giraffe then my confidence would have been high, I would surely have been released with no questioning, but I was not. My jump was being measured to see if I had the remotest chance of putting my hands in front of volleyballs leaving a Brazilian's hand at approximately thirteen feet in the air travelling at 80 miles an hour and stopping that ball from crossing the net.

My first jump would have afforded a pleasant view of the underside of those volleyballs. My second, would have allowed me to wave frantically at the ball and hope to create an updraft causing it to deviate out over the baseline and my third jump, although better, saw me crash down to the pavement below and land on all the other Penthouse hopefuls.

I was invited to a subsequent trial in Bristol. This I felt went well, I was on talking terms with a number of the top players and hung about with them all day to give the impression that I was in with the in crowd. The day passed pretty much without incident. My moments of glory came when I wiped off Phil Davies block, twice in a row, and he nodded a cursory acknowledgement of my shots. The trials were over and I had no indication that my chances were good.

So there I sat, hoping against hope that I was selected and letting my mind wander to four weeks in the Brazilian sun. It was time to open the envelope. Anyone that has had bad news by post will probably be able to empathise with me at this point. I opened the envelope and read in silence. Thank you, but no thank you. That was it, one minute on a plane soaring toward the samba music and the next sat in Hampshire on a substantially colder and darker November morning.

A couple of months later with the selected team having completed many weekends of training, Brazil was declared bankrupt and the Games was cancelled. When I heard the news it made the earlier disappointment fade, but I can honestly say that I really felt bad for the players. Much more cruel to take the prize away just before it is due to be unwrapped.

Sava time..................

All that was left for me, following the student team rejection, was to pursue my Division 1 NVL career with Capital City Spikers. Still completely new to the team and to Division One the challenge was exciting and motivated me to work very hard for my chances.

The team was on the way down from the dizzy heights it had achieved only seasons earlier, when it could start many England squad players like Neville and Denton McKenzie, Rob Kittlety, Phil Davies, Steve Rodd and Brian Donelon. The only remaining players from that period were the brilliant Neville McKenzie and Andy Fuller, an incredibly underrated player of the time. Neville, nicknamed 'Lucifer' for his powerful hitting, was nowhere near his best. A best that had brought him to the attentions of the Moscow Dynamo coach. While on a students playing trip to the Soviet Union, Neville was spotted at a scrimmage game against a lower division team and invited to train with Dynamo, the KGB sports club, for the evening. This invite meant that he had the pleasure of working alongside volleyball greats like Savin, Sorokolet and the setter Zaitsev, one of my all time heroes.

Prior to the 1988 season though Neville had undergone shoulder surgery which was forcing him to hit left handed. Because of this he had decided he wanted to continue volleyball, but only as a setter.

The former England men's coach, Sava Medonos, had returned to

Capital City for the season and he had signed the former Team Wiles Travel and University of British Columbia setter, Neil Withington. I just sort of stumbled into the team, desperate to play Div 1 and turning up on a tentative invite from England and British student player Graham McConney. It was my usual bit of luck, I was in the right place at the right time, with a good bunch of lads to show me the ropes. Players like Geoff Waterman and the now London Volleyball Association Chairman, Jonathan Doyle.

That whole season was an incredible experience, I learned so much. We were eventually demoted to division two, when Redwood Lodge, another now defunct club appealed against our league win over them due to a late switch of venue. The E.V.A upheld their appeal and we went down. Despite that, the season was a terrific one.

Sava was and is a real volleyball character. He gave absolutely no quarter to the team and quickly lost two key players, mainly through his eastern European philosophy with regard to the autocratic nature of his coaching and extreme physical demands of his sessions. Only a few games in Graham McConney and Neville McKenzie transferred out of the squad. Graham went to the improving Star Aquila and Neville left to understudy Richard Dobell, the new wonder-boy of British volleyball who had transferred that year from Staffordshire Moorlands.

I travelled many miles with Sava to and from training, he taught me a lot about the sport and I could listen to his fascinating volleyball stories for hours.

Sava Medonos was a former Czechoslovakian senior international. If we wanted success badly enough, he would be more than happy to push us to our limits. He came from a background of tortuous training sessions and a hard knocks international system. He had played when volleyball, even in winter, was an outdoor sport. No shit! Sava had played internationals against the USSR, Bulgaria and Hungary on a court laid out on the gravel area at the top end of his countries national football stadium, in front of twenty thousand spectators. The Russian game was played just prior to the Soviet Union's invasion of Czechoslovakia in 1968, only weeks later Sava defected to Sweden and then eventually England.

He was forty five years old when he coached us, with knee problems from his national squad days. He always took sessions in smart trousers and a shirt and tie, trainers being his only concession to his evening job as a sports coach. He was always incredibly intense and despite his knee pain would occasionally lose it with the hitters at sessions and with no warm-up leap up and lamp the living crap out of the ball, shouting.
"Bloody hell! like this, like this."

As a coach he gave a tremendous amount and demanded that commitment be returned by the players. He had no second thoughts when it came to put-

42

ting his players through painful drills, believing it was the only way to develop character. To his credit he would, again with no warm-up, demonstrate certain difficult manoeuvres to show the players he was part of the team. Sava's claim to fame was his six hook serve aces that he served against the Soviet Union in a friendly, if that was the word, international. I remember the team talking him into showing us one of these legendary serves. He fizzed one over and aced us. From there Sava got into a euphoric rhythm and we battled it out with him for several minutes. Just as quickly as he started, he stopped and told everyone to take a drink, then shouted. "Mr Golding, come over here please."

I jogged over to him and asked what he wanted, fearing maybe I was to demonstrate a new and even more lung busting drill to the team. "You have a sports degree, yes ?" Sava asked. I nodded. "Well please look at this and tell me what you think it is."

He rolled up his shirt sleeve and held out his arm. It was a little confusing to start with, but then it became clearer. Sava had detached part of his biceps tendon from his lower arm and was showing me a golf ball sized lump that was protruding from the biceps area on his upper arm. He must have been in absolute agony, but he insisted I tell no one, then continued with session and dropped in to casualty on the way home.

Although not a sensible course of action and risking serious long term damage, it is behaviour like that which can tend to be very humbling and not a little unnerving.

Sava sometimes seemed like, but was not really, a complete bastard. He loved volleyball and had tremendous respect for any player that worked hard for him. I once cut my chin badly in one of his drills, but continued through to the end. He sprinted up to me after the drill beaming all over his face, with a tear in his eye and clasped his arm tight around my shoulder. Shaking me from side to side, blood now covering my shirt, he shouted in his broad European accent.

"Yes! Mr Golding (he called everybody by their surname) you are bleeding, well done, I am proud of you."

Sava's great and abiding talent was for story telling, always told in his strong accent, with gleaming wide eyes and great guffawing laughter and accelerated speech at the conclusion of each tale. He recounted tales about the long haired Bulgarians with one metre standing jumps who wore their hair up in crocheted woollen skull caps. He told me about one of his team mates who was doing extra weights, in his student hostel, against the coaches wishes. The player was using a metal bar with buckets of cement on each end on a bench press, he dropped the bar across his neck and nearly killed himself.

My favourite anecdotes though, show that sport doesn't change as much as we may think. Although undeniably different from decade to decade, basic human behaviours continue.

The Czech team were mostly young students and played internationals on a regular basis. Over time the team realised they had a group devoted female fans that turned up to games. In particular there were two young women who had begun to hang about at practice and show up in the restaurant after games, to socialise with the players.

The coach began to notice the young women and their positive effect on the team. In the next home international, much to the team's surprise, he invited the girls to sit on the teams wooden bench by the side of the court. The move inspired the team to greater acrobatics.

It is an amazing male phenomenon, but when women show up a at a local sports venue the male participants are immediately drawn to strenuous exertions. It must be an ancient genetic code that kicks in, but if the female of the species appears on a sports hall balcony the male badminton players, soccer players and basketball players begin to attempt some gut wrenching gymnastic manoeuvres.

The Czech team were no different. The Captain, who from Sava's descriptions seemed to be Captain due to the fact that he was the one most likely to end up covered in blood by the end of the match, was excelling himself in defence. The young women were clearly enjoying the spectacle and shouted excitedly from the bench, much to the crowds amusement.

The innocence of the whole idyllic picture was just about to be shattered though. The Captain began an almost suicidal chase for a ball shanked towards the stand by one of his team . He went after the ball (remember Sava is cranking it up now, building to the finish) which was floating away from court directly over the Czech bench. The team, the coach and the trainer, all old volleyball lags knew the routine. Leave the bench fast and get out of the Captain's way. The young women were not old lags by any stretch of the imagination, so they just remained seated on the bench, gazing in awe at the Captain now heading straight for them.

The ball began to drop and the Captain threw himself headlong towards it. He made contact with the ball, but as he passed over the bench he caught a piece of it with his trailing leg. The bench tipped over, taking it's female occupants with it. The girls were thrown backwards and their legs and consequently their skirts were thrown back over their heads and as Sava shouted at the end of the story.

"Bloody hell! they had no knickers on!"

Sava's other great story simply shows that the practice of getting a laugh out of the new kids on a team is as old as volleyball itself. The Czech team recruited a new setter who made the starting six very quickly. They were in the changing rooms prior to a major international, the new setter was sat nervously in the corner. The weather was freezing outside, with sleet and biting winds. One of the primary concerns for the new setter was how to warm his hands up for the game.

In came the Captain, with a benevolent look on his face. He had a tray in his hands, balanced on the tray was a pile of horse shit, steaming in the cold changing room air. The Captain told the setter it was the only thing that would work to warm his hands and the team's last setter swore by it. The young setter glanced around the room and his gaze was met by the team nodding wisely. They could barely contain themselves as he stood up and plunged his hands into the pile of horse manure, which was greeted by howls of laughter.

At Capital City I was keen to succeed and responded completely to the training environment as did Neil Withington and Andy Fuller. The training really was hard. Players used to be sick fairly regularly after and during some drills. Drills in which you thought your chest would explode, when you finished barely able to stand. These drills comprised the bulk of all Sava's coaching work. No technical information would pass his lips until we were physically ready to act on it. The effect of this improved fitness for some players therefore was the ability to make the same old mistakes, but for much longer and with more power.

Therein lay the eternal problem for Sava and his work with English volleyball. He came from such a tough volleyball background that English efforts must have looked relatively pathetic. He met his wife when she was assigned to him by the national squad at Prague University, as his running partner. His wife was an international swimmer in her own right, but after her practice at 7.30am everyday of the season, except Sunday, Sava would have to collect her from the pool and run with her on his back twice around the campus (4 miles). Then drop her off at breakfast. Rain, snow or shine. That is how they got to know each other.

The Czech coaching staff would physically and verbally assault the players if they were not happy with the team effort and make them suffer in drills, if any player dared show descent. Their games were played on gravel, sometimes just after they had been cleared of snow. The English dedication to avoiding hard work on the volleyball court appalled Sava and frequently drove him to distraction. The only other parallels in English volleyball would be some of the Polish coaches that Polonia have hired over the years. Coaches like Edeck Len who was famous for his phrase.

"If you don't do it I will get my gun and shoot you!"

Basically, even the hard workers in his English teams, including Sava's spell as National coach, just did not compare to the work he had put in and

45

witnessed from many great players of his past.

When he originally came to England he took over as coach of a third division team in Kent. They were all pretty new to the sport. Sava got them a sponsorship with a travel agency and put them all to work. In his first season they won division three easily and sent shock waves through volleyball when they turned over the league Division 1 champions Polonia at the Tachikara tournament.

Capital City saw Sava as the way forward and lured him away from Team Wiles, the Wiles players never really forgave him. Within months of starting with Capital City, England appointed him as the new coach. This is where the problems began. He was now working with players who would challenge his word, his judgements and his coaching methods. The culture clash was evidently not pretty.

Sava began to despair, following his first England session, players began to find excuses not to attend or to miss the fitness work. One player even turned up late for session two, claiming his dog had died. Sava's stock expression was 'Bloody Hell!' which sounded more like 'blurdy hail!' when he shouted it. Sava would recount this story on many occasions."On the third session, the same player was late again" Sava would exclaim, still completely indignant about the event, years later.

"He came in and told me again, 'I'm sorry I'm late, but my dog has died'. Bloody Hell I shouted and began to leave the gym. The player asked where I was going and I told him. I am going to phone the R.S.P.C.A and report you for killing your pets!"

Weeks after that the E.V.A contacted Sava to suggest he should temper his approach at exactly the same time as the Capital City players requested the same thing. Sava told them it was 'he' that told them what to do, not the other way around and he was now telling them that he quit.

Now he was back with a fresh crop of players and he pushed us hard every Tuesday and Thursday, some of us responded. By November of that year I had moved to the Isle of Sheppey in order to work and train with Neil Withington the team setter and a player who was as ambitious as myself, with regard to volleyball.

The changing point in our physical ability happened at around this time. However, it is also the period of time that cost me the health of my right shoulder and eventually as my retirement testifies the cartilage in my knees.

Capital City sessions under Sava could be murderous. They tended to keep to a format which Sava had developed from several sources, but most notably the infamous Japanese system of the 1960's under Matsudaira, a coach that Sava worshipped.

The session started with a warm-up, no problem. Then the following activities prior to the session proper. Do not attempt these with your teams.

1. Pair of players tap smash between each other, one player working for ten repetitions and then swap over. Each separate drill required the players to complete two sets of ten repetitions.
a) Smash at your partner. The partner digs back to you then dives to one side, recovers their position and makes the next dig and dive. Repeat ten times on a left dive then the right.
b) Same routine as a), but dive forwards for ten then roll backwards for ten.
2. Fifty jumps with a basketball at the net, throwing two handed over the net and into court.
3. The clock drill. The player sits on a bag in the middle of a circle of play- ers 6 players. The first feeder drops the ball and the player working sprints and dives out to make an extreme recovery. Stands up and sprints back to the bag, sits down and repeats the same action but to the next player, twice around the clock and two sets overall.

After those we would begin to train. Then at the end of the session we would always finish with my favourite drill. Sava had a volleyball full of lead shot attached to a swivel with a long section of thick rope tied to that. This was straight out of the Japanese manual and I loved it, many did not.

Sava would get on his knees and whirl the rope and ball in a big circle around his body , about three feet off of the floor. The first few weeks it was like skipping and everyone liked it. Get in, make ten jumps and get out. Then came the sting. Players were invited to make one jump then one dive over the swinging rope. That was when it started to get hairy. Sava did not know it, but I had a copy of the Japanese manual. The Japanese players, Sato, Oko and the incredible Nekoda would do somersaults over the rope. We never got to that level, but some of us could make ten jumps and ten dives all in one visit after several weeks practice. Some players just hurt themselves every week.

I talked to an old Team Wiles player not long ago and we compared Sava drills. The weighted ball came up as the first point of discussion.

"Did he used to use that black leather glove to hold the rope while he was swinging the ball round?" he asked.

I confirmed that Sava always used to put the glove on prior to the drill with an almost Machevellian touch.

"Yeh! we used to gob in that glove." he laughed.

The regular sessions then closed with sprints. Ten sprints to start with, for the whole team. Then the races. If you won the race you could stop. In the midst of this bi-weekly torture Sava decided that Neil, Andy and myself were coping and could step up to the next level, the legendary 'Cuban session'.

It was rumoured that Sava, while in Sweden, had been given a copy of the Cuban jump programme that had enabled many Cuban players to develop their outstanding leaping ability. In a very sombre meeting with Sava he handed over the Cuban session, individually copied out for each of us and made us promise to secrecy. We did so and took away the information as if it were gold dust.

The session was for both upper body and legs and it took around one and a half hours to complete. The upper body stuff was sound, but the leg work was sickening, it really was murder. We did it religiously, three times a week. For the first two month we suffered severe over-training, struggling to train in between the sessions. Such was our respect for Sava we kept going and although we began to deal with the demands of the Cuban session it was still a difficult regime to follow. The leg work consisted of the following drills.

The Cuban Session

1. 3 sets of two minutes continuous rebound block jumps to a mark 80% of your full jump.
2. 3 sets of maximum one leg jumps, right then left.
3. 3 sets of ten standing calf raises with 100% body weight.
4. 3 sets of ten jump squats at 80% body weight.
5. 3 sets to failure, full squats 100% body weight.

The whole thing was obscenely tough. Our performances went downhill for some time, but towards the end of the season and through the summer my jump heights and hitting power began to increase dramatically. I still would not ever recommend this approach to any player however. After a few months I was physically stronger than I had ever been and was beginning to jump and hit like some of my heroes in division 1.

The World Student Games, Sheffield 1991.
My second attempt.........................

In January 1989, after giving up a job in recruitment consultancy something I was truly rubbish at, I moved to the Isle of Sheppey. Neil Withington had a job for me in the recreation centre he worked at, in Sheerness. Neil's parents very kindly offered me a room in their house at peppercorn rent, for which I will always be grateful. It meant that I was able to travel to London twice a week with Neil to train at Capital City while working at the rec centre which gave me free access to a weights room. It was a really good set up for my first year out of College and enabled me to continue towards my goal of competing in the 1991 World Student Games.

The only unusual thing about staying with Neil's parents was Neil's Dad, Mike. He is a great bloke, generous to a fault, but also ex-navy and very much of the 'bring back National Service for the youth' era. He was close to retirement when I was living with them and had always been proud of his fitness and was working as a prison officer in one of the local establishments.

Mike kept fit at various circuit sessions per week and wasn't happy unless he had a certain amount of hardship or challenge in his life. The challenges came from demonstrating his still considerable strength against Neil and myself. Coming back to the house after a shift at the centre was a bit like Inspector Clouseau coming back to his apartment and being set upon by Kato. You walked through the front door and into the house and crept carefully through to the kitchen, Mike could attack at any minute. He would jump out on you and explain that he had been taught a new move at work today to control a violent prisoner one on one. He then confirmed that you were now taking on the role of prisoner, even if you didn't want to. Most of these moves, in fact all of these moves, involved Mike grabbing your fingers or thumbs and bending them to unnatural angles while shouting.
"See, I've got you, you can't do anything can you!"

I would nod my agreement and he would let me go then talk casually about how my day had gone and how volleyball was progressing. Neil was another story altogether, he used to fight back. Huge physical fights would develop and move through the kitchen and into the lounge where Neil's Mum, Pat, would sometimes be sitting watching the television. With years of experience of these incidents she would be completely oblivious to Neil and his Dad giving it full WWF through the house. Occasionally she would say in a resigned manner.
"Out the way of the television boys."

I used to look on in wonder. These play fights looked dangerous and I would often look on in horror as Mike bent Neil's fingers this way and that. Neil would grab him back and they would lurch around laughing. Neil was the only setter Capital City had so I'm sure Sava would have been less that pleased at their antics.

My oyher fond memory was of Mike's enforced weekly hardship. This was more bizarre than the 'let me show you my latest hold' episodes. Each morning come sun, rain or snow, Mike would take himself back to his navy days. They lived in a lovely house in Minster on the island, with all modern facilities and a nice bathroom. Mike though, liked to do his morning ablutions in the conservatory at 6.00am, semi-naked in a bucket of freezing cold water. I would come down to breakfast for the early shift at the sport centre, just after he had finished in the conservatory, having taken a lovely warm shower upstairs. I'll never forget Mike just staring at me like I was some soft bastard for using the house facilities.

British Championships, Weston-Super-Mare 1989 and the Germans............

In the Easter of 1989 Neil and Myself were contacted by Keith Nicholls, it appeared that both of us were invited to play in the British Students team in the forthcoming British Championships. The British Volleyball Federation had invited the students in, as preparation for the 1991 World Students games. We joined the team for training the week prior to the 1989 Championships held at Woodsmoor Leisure Centre in Weston Super-mare. It truly was the last year of volleyball innocence in Britain, Nick Moody coaching Scotland and Jefferson Williams still a new phenomenon coaching England and only months before the arrival of Ralph Hippolyte.

We had a great time. The team piled into Weston on the Friday night and ended up in a pub on the sea front, which was distinctly dodgy, but at least they let us in. The pub was holding a German night. There was a German band and all the regulars were dressed in German costumes. We initially thought it was mostly restricted to a beer festival atmosphere and traditional German folk dress, lederhosen etc. We quickly noticed however, that there were an alarming number of regulars dressed as nazi's and some had gone as far as donning some Hitler garb. With the surname Golding I was uncomfortable with the set up to say the least, but we also had two Polonia with us Chris Leshniak and Chris Hykiel, who found it offensive. But a beer is a beer is a beer, so we stayed in to observe.

Chris Hykiel is six foot eight and without fail, whenever we go out, he attracts comments about his height. That night was no exception and he had one local after another use the same phrase on him.

"'Ere youm a big bastard int you."

Chris nodded a tired agreement to keep them sweet, because there is nothing like a small bloke with a chip on his shoulder who wants to have a pop at a big guy. The evening went on and before we knew it the regulars were starting to do their version of German folk dancing. We were dragged into very reluctant action and instructed to form two lines, which ran the

50

length of the pub, through which the locals could cavort (German style). They danced gaily back and forth, some as it emerged danced more gaily than others. Chris was standing next to me and began to look perplexed. I asked him what the problem was. He shouted over the accordion music that one particularly small chap, who was very light on his feet, was making a discreet grab for Chris's crown jewels on every prance past.

Chris Leshniak the other Polish player had also had his meat and two veg given the once over by the now smiling pervert. He was now positively beaming at his good fortune, he looked like Dale Winton let loose in a men's volleyball changing room.

Both Chris's had had enough and on the little chaps next dance by as he left a stray hand around Chris Hykiel's toilet department, Chris stuck out a foot and tripped him. The bloke stumbled and as he went past Chris Leshniak, an incredibly physically strong individual, he gave him a very hearty German style slap across the back. The little man, no longer smiling continued his stumble, but now at a vastly increased pace. He shot down the line and smashed through the swing door of the ladies lavatories, ending up on the floor. The pub went quiet. The music stopped. The landlord, jet black hair, big side parting, small moustache marched over to us.

"There is no need for that lads." He said.

Chris went to defend himself, but the landlord did not want to hear his protestations. The team made a unilateral and publicity conscious withdrawal.

Myself and the team had a fantastic time. I got to play most of the tournament and we ended up beating the Republic of Ireland for a bronze medal. I was definitely hooked on the students set up and the idea of Sheffield, fuelled by missing out on Sao Paulo. My on court play got a write up from Clive Ellis in E.V.A volleyball magazine of the time.

Having enjoyed the British Championships experience, my World Student Games flame was rekindled. With Sheffield 1991 in mind I applied to return to my old college to top up my existing degree and thus make myself eligible for two more years of student volleyball.

During the summer immediately after my first division one season the Capital City team were invited to a tournament in Belgium that Sava used to go to many years ago. It was my first shot at European volleyball and was to be my first encounter with foreign teams.

We prepared thoroughly for the tournament and Neil and I packed our kit on the Friday before departure on the ferry that afternoon. We got into Neil's car to drive to Dover and as I sat down in the passenger seat Neil laughingly said, "packed your passport ?"

Passport! Did we need a passport for Belgium? Surely we were jolly good friends with the Belgians. Neil confirmed we did need a passport. We had some four hours before departure and my passport was in Southampton, a good six hour round trip away.

I wandered back into the house with the kind of irrational feelings that we as young people get, churning round my head. With the benefit of age and countless experiences it so much easier to reflect on situations that challenge us, usually because we have a similar experience to reflect on and a equally calming memory of how we sorted it out.

When I broke my leg playing football I firmly believed for days that I would never walk again, let alone play again and my girlfriend would dump me. I did walk again and she didn't dump me.

So, with no passport I was about to miss my trip to Belgium, no I was about to be denied my only chance of ever playing abroad. I would never get another chance. My depression began to deepen.

Neil's Dad walked in and matter-of-factly asked why I was slumped in his living room when I should have been heading to Dover. I told him that I had no passport and therefore I was stranded on the Isle of Sheppey for ever and would probably never ever go abroad again. He simply said, completely nonplussed by my amateur dramatics, that I would have to get a temporary passport. Temporary passport! Once he explained what that actually was the next few hours became like the last five minutes of Benny Hill show, without the scantily clad women. Neil and I flew around Sheerness, the main town on Sheppey getting my photos done and filling out forms. I eventually got the documentation and we made the ferry by the skin of our teeth.

The whole Belgian thing was an interesting experience. Teams were not stacked with massive players, but they were all technically superior to us, the result of hours of practice and playing from an early age. One player stood out a mile. He played for the local professional team and blessed with an incredible jump and some awesome hitting power. One level up from Banks and Mckenzie in York.

It emerged as the tournament went on that this supreme middle player was in fact a French 'B' squad international player. For the life of me I cannot remember his name. All I remember is Sava looking at the player and deciding that he had to sign him for Capital City. It was such an obvious plan, he was currently training with the French squad and getting a car, money and an apartment with his Belgian team. Almost no contest then. Sava could offer him no money, no apartment, no car and second division volleyball. The guy would have to be crazy to turn us down.

Sava went to speak to the player. At nearly fifty Sava was blessed with absolute confidence in his ability as a coach and with years of international playing experience behind him he had every right to be speaking to fellow international. Unfortunately Sava was also from Czechoslovakia, educated in a different culture and despite his experiences, not so Worldly wise. Sava was not a particularly good judge of people. He was unable to read the subtle nuances that so many of use as natural defensive mechanisms from people we don't want to get involved with or trust. The type of signals that we pick up which tell us whether the person we have just met is our type of person. Triumphantly Sava came over to us and called a meeting. He explained that he had secured the services of the French player for Capital City. All we had to do was get him a job and offer him a place to live. Essentially not to much of a problem.

Next step, French international meets team. He came over to us sporting a huge beatific smile. We smiled back and then it hit us, a factor that again was not essentially a problem, but a factor that Sava would never have picked up in a month Sundays.

Our French International was unbelievably camp. He began to chatter in excellent English and to a man we stood transfixed. Using expansive gestures he explained that he had many friends in London that he wanted to visit and playing for us would enable him to do that. I can only describe his general persona as Eddie Murphy stood at the reception to the 'posh' club in the film Beverly Hills Cop, saying "I need to see Victor, I have er....herpasimplex 10" in a clipped effeminate accent. The French guy though, was even more camp and excitable than that. You could see the players recalling Sava's original gems of information, the job was still not a problem, but who was Liberace going to live with?

Aside from that there was no doubt that he was a very talented player. He put on something of a display for the rest of the tournament, roofing players or hammering 'A-quick' attacks on the floor then turning to smile, wave and point at all of us assembled in the stands. His current team pissing themselves laughing and some even beginning to join in the waving and camp gestures.

To cut a long story short Sava never heard from him again and our French International never appeared.

I remained with Capital in division 2 and continued to get stronger and better as a player. I was now studying in Chichester again and Capital City were training in Sittingbourne in Kent, a 4 hour train ride, a night over on the isle of Sheppey and the train back. Twice a week. At the peak of my physical ability and playing good volleyball it was about to go wrong, not wrong to the point where I chucked it in, but the kind of wrong that in developed sports nations unlike our own, would never have happened.

I had been hitting hard at a training session one evening. I had continued to hit for a long time, working at a high intensity. I awoke the next morning to with a terrible pain in my right shoulder. I couldn't move my arm or even lift a cup of tea to my lips.

I headed straight to a hospital and received a stunning level of treatment. Four hours in casualty, in agony. An x-ray followed and I was told absolutely nothing was wrong and I was to rest it. The pain would probably go away. The pain did not go away, but I was desperate to play so I covered the injury up. I could still block and pass but could not swing my arm. I managed to hold my place and keep playing. Ridiculous really, I had torn my rotator cuff and should have rested and probably had surgery, but there is no easy access to treatment and I was petrified of taking time out from the game.

Years later my shoulder is still painful, it has got easier but never went away. I still get times when I simply cannot swing at the ball and I have never regained the hitting power I used to have. I managed to retain my places on various squads by working harder in defence, on block and as a passer.

A year after Weston-Super-Mare and following regular training camps, the student team headed off to Glasgow for the 1990 British Championships once more. The team was becoming more established and we had developed a good rapport within the squad. All the teams were based in the Stakis hotel just outside Glasgow and a short minibus ride from Kelvin Hall, where the tournament was to be held.

Pre-tournament training went reasonably well and we ended up in Sheffield for a training weekend. We trained hard for two days and come Sunday most of the players were tired, even the arrival of a Yorkshire T.V crew to film us for a 'special', did little to raise our game. The only players still with any energy were the fittest players in the team Roger Hunter and Neil Withington. Roger died in 1993 in a car accident, a terrible situation for his family, friends and Leeds his NVL team. It was also hard for his former student team mates to come to terms with the loss. I am sure we all think of Roger from time to time, I know when he passes through my thoughts I am often reminded of his never ending enthusiasm and one hundred percent effort. These qualities appealed to the Director who attended our session with his film crew, they were also the qualities which eventually destroyed the session.

The director came in to the gym in a big semi-Caftan shirt and a flowing silk scarf draped loosely around his neck. John Lyall our manager called us in to be addressed by the Director. John introduced the man and then made a couple of comments by way of an explanation. He told us that the crew were making a film for the Games and the needed to film various bits of the competing sports to make a sequence. The Director looked at John like he was a hopeless amateur valiantly stumbling through a guided tour on a film set and walked forward and touched John on the shoulder and hushed him up.

"What John is trying to say is" he began with a patronising tone and an ostentatious smile, indicating his undoubted artistic flare. He sounded just like Kenneth Williams.

"We are putting together a vignette, a montage if you will."

"Yeh! that's what I said, various bits of sports to make a sequence." chipped in John, a no nonsense Scotsman who hadn't enjoyed being 'handled' by the Director.

"Yes." replied the Director, now slightly put out, betraying his annoyance with a withering look at John. He continued.

"My vision is to produce a piece which off sets the various activities against each other, today we shall capture hand on leather, then head off to the fencing session for metal on metal."

The Director had watched some of the training and knew that he was after shots of the setter setting and the hitter spiking the resulting set. The crew took another hour to set up and when they were ready we did another warm-up and got ourselves ready for 'action'. The Director called us in again and informed us we were to ignore him and the crew, pretend that they weren't there. Mr Spielberg knew what he wanted for his first shot and he wanted Neil.

"You first." he drawled seductively pointing at Neil, who shifted nervously from foot to foot where he stood. "I want you to throw yourself on the floor."

The shot was set up and Neil, master of the swallow dive, launched a fantastic effort. The Director clapped excitedly and shouted "Yes! Yes! and again."

Neil dived again and as he stood up the Director rushed over to help him off the floor.

"Oooh! does that hurt?" he was enquiring.

Next shot was to be the set and spike. He wanted Neil again, there was a pattern developing, he also liked the look of Roger and summoned him as the spiker. It would have been OK! if he had asked the players in those volleyball terms, unfortunately for Roger and Neil he chose to embarrass them in front of all of us.

"You I want to tippy the ball up in the air and you to run in and bash it as hard as you can." He said. We were giggling now.

The shot was set up and Roger fed the ball in to Neil, Neil 'tippied' the ball up as best he could and Roger came steaming in and absolutely 'bashed' it, boy did he bash it. We watched delighted as the ball skidded off the floor and demolished the film crew's lighting rig with a loud crash, bulbs exploded and bits flew high in the air all rounded off with a gentle tinkling of glass. It took another half hour to put the lighting back together, the Director had to walk away to compose himself, Roger and the rest of us were spoken to by a flustered production assistant. We tried to listen and look serious as she explained that Roger had just caused over five hundred pounds worth of damage, Roger didn't try as hard as the rest of us and stood there smiling proudly.

The next shot was predictably a cameraman laying on the floor and filming up between Neil's legs as we jumped over the prostrate crew member to hit spikes. It was destined to disaster and we were now in a gung ho mood after the lights incident and the Directors obvious increasing dissatisfaction. We hauled our tired bodies in to hit, I barely made it over the cameraman catching his jeans with my trainers. All of us came too close for comfort. Then the last man in the queue Chris Hykiel shuffled in to hit, the genuine intention to jump was there, the actual ability to leave the floor for any amount of time wasn't. Chris jumped, just, connected with the ball and landed right on the cameraman's groin. The team and coaches were laughing as the poor cameraman rolled around the floor holding his tackle and groaning, the Director stormed off and never returned. We never saw the piece.

British Championships, Glagow 1990. Scotland, England, Ireland and....... Whales.

The team began to get the hang of how training camps and tournaments should run and in what had previously been boring gaps between workouts and games we started to do team stuff. Eating, shopping, watching films and playing other sports like golf and ten pin bowling. One particular attempt at golf produced a remarkable escape from injury for the whole team.

We had all gone to the golf driving range in the Stakis hotel grounds in Glasgow, the day before our first game in the 1990 British Championships. The players were lined up in the driving booths and those of us that had played before were swinging away already. Some players were not at all familiar with golf, this included six foot eight Polonia player, Chris Hykiel. Chris was stood with a seven iron, the first time he had held a golf club. He was staring at it like detective Colombo holding a murder weapon. Little did we know.

Alex Gunn, the Scottish middle blocker and an excellent golf player in his own right, gave Chris a few pointers and then left him to it. Chris was situated in the middle of all of us and stood pondering the simple advice he had been given.

I was recently treated to a description of Joe Mildred's legendary golf style, by Grant Pursey. The description induced one of the best laughing fits I have had in ages and reminded me of Chris.

Due to Chris's height the seven iron was just not long enough for him.

To get any kind of proximity of club head to ball he had splayed his legs out either side of his body, knees together then lower legs almost at right angles. He looked much less like Ernie Els and far more like a giraffe trying to lick a marshmallow off the floor. The players gradually stopped and began to focus on the mammoth effort Chris was making to form a position that might allow him to strike the ball. He was splaying his legs and craning over the ball, holding the golf club like a baseball bat. His first three swings and misses started us all off, after the next three we were crying with laughter.

Then it happened, the most miraculous escape since the A-Team were last locked in a garage with just a tractor, a welding torch, some sheet steel and a crate of dynamite.

Chris took an almighty swing, the effort was immense and the look of determination on his face added to the comedy. If he had missed again I and no doubt some of us would have wet our trousers. He did not miss though, he connected. He connected, but with the toe of the club. The ball, invisible to the naked eye at that speed, shot off the tee sideways. The golf booths were constructed from round steel poles and rails. The ball was only distinguishable from the ping! noise it made on every pole it contacted, the only pole it did not hit was Chris.

The ball ricocheted back and forth between the booths at shin and head height depending on the angle that it struck the round poles at. It made it's perilous way along the booths. The occupants, namely us, remained absolutely frozen and silent. The ball missed everyone, I still don't know how and gradually lost it's momentum before stopping.

We all stood, amazed. Mike Rhodes was the first to speak, his simple 'fuck me!' summed it up.

The tournament was OK! but as a team we played badly. We slogged it out with Wales for a three nil win and another Bronze medal and Scotland in front of a partisan home support to the championships from England in the final. With Paul Carruthers unstoppable for Scotland. It was also the first chance that we had to look at the teenager Matt Jones, plucked from third division obscurity weeks earlier and called up for England. Boy's Own stuff.

The celebrations in the Stakis that night were awesome. Phil Newton who had set some of the final for England was on the piano and Scotland, England, Wales, Northern Ireland and the Republic of Ireland were on incredibly drunk vocals.

The reason we were providing the entertainment was that the disco had packed up and gone home in a fit of pique. This fit of pique was induced by myself, Stewart Fullerton, Donald Deans and Graham McConney (all with seat cushions crammed down the back of our trousers) dancing in front of the disco and insisting on doing 'disco style' soul turns every time Stewart

Fullerton shouted.

"Soul turn!"

The music stopped and a balding Glaswegian D.J with halitosis and no sense of humour stepped out from behind his decks. Cheered on by the assembled players he screamed at us.

"If you bastards don't stop taking the piss, I'm gonna pack up and go home and you'll have ruined it for the rest."

We tried to look suitably contrite, but as if tempting fate the silly sod put on 'don't blame it on the boogie' by the Jackson Five. We were goaded into action and once again our leader Stewart shouted his command and we obeyed. The needle scratched across the record, the D.J pulled the plug and we adjourned to the lounge and the grand piano.

I witnessed many things that night. The Scots know how to have a great time, we got bladdered, while being entertained by the likes of John Lyle (the students manager) and one of the biggest characters in British volleyball history Mr John Scringeour.

The stories I have heard about sweem could fill another book. My only real contact with the man was on court at the Scottish Open in Perth. I had made the journey up to sell T-shirts at the tournament in the days when I airbrushed shirts for a living. I was on court for Kilmarnock, then West Coast, playing in the middle. On the opposite side of the net for Dundee was Sweem. "Hey! I know you." Said Sweem with a friendly smile.

I smiled back at him, genuinely touched that a Scottish volleyball legend such as him should acknowledge my lowly presence on court.

"Yep! you're that wee poofty bastard who paints the T-shirts, aren't ya!" he added. Then for the duration of the game proceeded to make me look like a complete idiot novice.

Back to the Stakis and the Scots were in great form. John Lyle insisted he was a whale about every half an hour and following an elaborate build up would spray beer across the audience, out of his imaginary blow hole mouth.

On our way up to our rooms at the end of the night, we found John face down on the hotel stairs. I pulled his head up to check he was all right and he smiled with his eyes closed and uttered quietly, "I'm a whale."

The most memorable moment of the night for me was seeing Ralph Hippolyte the soon to be guru of British volleyball. He was on his first trip to Britain and had collapsed, drunk (or jet lagged), in an armchair in the bar. He had been surrounded by sycophants for most of the evening, but when we found him he was completely on his own and completely out of it.

I and some other students approached him. He had his clipboard and pen on his lap. Firstly I took his clipboard and wrote on it 'Simon Golding is brilliant, pick him.' Then I wrote down my address. I didn't know it, but this was to be my first and only contact with Ralph. I never was picked, not because of the clipboard incident, but because I wasn't good enough and he never ever spoke to me.

Ralph still didn't move and I could not resist it. I got my camera and a serviette and got one of the other student players to photograph me polishing his already shiny bald dome of a head.

At this point I would love to be writing see photograph opposite, but I lent it to someone years ago and it disappeared. So you will just have to believe me.

Whitfield, 1990. The arrival of the cavalry..........

Such was the team spirit at Glasgow that on returning to England, in a moment of euphoria, I entered the students into the Whitfield tournament as the 'Ambassadors' in the division of honour.

I had kit sponsorship sorted from my Dad's company SG Furnaces (some of you will still have one of those shirts somewhere) and courtesy of the squad dropping out one by one, the week prior to the tournament, no players. Ever the optimist I turned up at Whitfield with Neil, Nigel Stockhill and Calvin Morriss, confident we could field a team by dragging 'Ambassador' hopefuls off of the outdoor courts. Ever the optimist I was sat in the changing rooms at Bath university, with Neil, Nigel and Calvin and nine shirts, no other players.

There was about fifteen minutes to go before our first match of the tournament, against Aquila. The only other student player that had agreed to show up was I guy called Pepe D'iasso. There was still no sign of him.

Then the changing room door swung open and in walked Pepe. He stood and looked at me. "Is it true we've only got five ?" he said, looking serious, but really just heightening the dramatic tension for his own pleasure. "I don't know if they are any good, but I found a couple of lads on the train on the way down and they're looking for a team." he added.

I was happy to accept anyone that would bring us up to our regulation six. Pepe opened the door and in the walked. First in was the Scottish national squad setter Kenny Milne and Pepe became my instant best friend. We were sorted. But, in true 'and there's more' style, two more lads entered the changing rooms, Marek Banasiewicz, six foot nine, England international and then professional player with Fortuna Bonn in the German first division) followed by Dave Kalugerovic, six foot eight, (another Scottish international). It was unbelievable, like Christmas in July, the changing room was suddenly a cramped space.

Out we went with our ringers and proceeded to absolutely steam roller everyone. Banasiewicz was huge and almost unstoppable. Kalugerovic was a monster, a one man passing machine and exponent of the most devastating inside to out line shot you could ever hope to hit. With Withington and Milne, both solid hitters, operating a two setter system we were solid.

We dispatched Speedwell, Liverpool and Aquila on the Saturday. On Sunday we really turned it on in the semi-final and beat Polonia fifteen nil, fifteen one. By the final the 'Ambassador' players were flagging and Prague were too good. We went down three one, but that was a secondary consideration bearing in mind our predicament at 8.45am on Saturday.

After the game the Prague players sauntered over and eyed our playing shirts. They asked to swap, so we did in true international style. What a bloody scam. The Prague shirts on closer inspection were held together by the collar and badge and little else. They were very old, they looked like those old garments you see framed and mounted at museums. I stupidly put my pride and joy shirt in the washing machine, an hour later I pulled out the badge and what was left of the collar, the rest had disintegrated.

Perth, 1990. Bladdered and benched, big style...........

In the summer of 1990 I had applied to and been accepted on a coaching degree at Moray House in Edinburgh, with the idea that I was going to head up to Scotland and play with Edinburgh Jets. In actuality I never accepted my place and chose to stay down in England and start an art business. I had played in Scotland at several tournaments with various teams and had always had a great time up there. With this in mind and the possibility that I would be moving north, I contacted Jim Wylie the Edinburgh Jets coach who invited me up to play for Jets at the Scottish Open in Perth that summer. Perth is a fantastic tournament to play and I have made the trip on several occasions. Including one terrible time when I set off with Freddie in our Bedford Rascal van, top speed fifty five MPH. Freddie dozed off after we had filled up in a petrol station outside Birmingham and left me to navigate. I still don't know how it happened, but five hours of driving later I needed to stop for a wee and more petrol. I went up to the counter to pay for the fuel and the attendant said "Hello again Sir. Getting through some driving today then!"

I looked at him blankly and then recognised his face. I asked where I was and told me I was in a petrol station just outside Birmingham, for the second time that day. I had driven up the motorway, somehow turned around and then turned again, to end up at square one. The result, apart from a really annoyed girlfriend, Southampton to Perth in sixteen hours.

In 1990 it was only twelve hours on coaches and I finally got to Perth. The Jets team was an established outfit with several internationals in their ranks, it was a chance for an excellent weekends volleyball and I had been looking forward to the event for some ages. I knew the lads reasonably well and it was good to meet up with them again.

I checked into the team hotel and wandered down to the strange dome shaped 'Bells Sport Centre' where the main courts were situated. I popped my head round the door and took a look at the massive main hall set up for the tournament. I soon as I saw the courts I got the buzz and set off back to the hotel to meet up with the team for a meal.

We all ate in the hotel and we were under strict instructions not to drink too much or stay up late. The Jets players after their showing in Glasgow earlier that year were perfectly capable of having much too good a time. They were however very restrained and took up a place in the hotel bar. I enjoyed a great evening talking and laughing about a whole range of things. The players stated that I was the guest and didn't have to buy a drink, they would take care of it. I should have been suspicious I guess, but I had completely relaxed in their company and accepted their hospitality.

The team agreed to restrict it's first night intake to four pints each. I was still a student and although not able to afford four pints, I was completely able to consume them with no after affects. The pints arrived, all four as agreed, and I drank them. Each time a new pint arrived the purchaser of the beer would put the glass in front of me, look around the table a shout 'depth charge!' The other players would all reply with laughs and further shouts of depth charge. I mistakenly felt that this was some sort of team call and decided to join in. I must have looked as out of place as the Harry Enfield character from the big house joining his gardener Ted for a drink with Ted's mates. Sixteen Scots shouting 'depth charge!' and one confused Englishman, some seconds after, joining in with the shout.

The beer tasted strange, but delicious. I asked one of the players next to me about the unusual taste he told me, with a loud slow delivery and the other players listening in, that is was the peat that they used in the brewing process. Then there was a pause as I digested the gem of information, the players leaned in. "OK!" I smiled and nodded my acceptance of the peat theory. There was yet more laughter and another pint arrived.

It got to eleven and true to their word the team got up said their goodnights and left for bed. I attempted to get up and follow them, something didn't feel right. I had been caught up in the convivial atmosphere of the night, a guest player enjoying the wonderful of hospitality of his future team. Under those circumstances you rarely feel the affects of alcohol or take a mental note of whether another pint is a good idea or not. In my complete innocence

I had trusted my 'team mates' with my pre tournament well being. Why was it then that I could barely walk. I concentrated very hard on taking steps, but with no real success, my legs were not working particularly well.

I shuffled outside for a breath of fresh highland air. The air hit me and now I really couldn't walk and I also felt incredibly dizzy. I staggered back into the hotel and somehow found my way up the stairs and along towards my hotel room. Halfway down the corridor I came face to face with the Jets coach, Jim Wylie. His sage and humourless advice to 'take it easy tonight lads' rang in my ears. He asked if I had enjoyed the evening. I nodded hoping against hope that he would be happy with that and toddle off to bed. He didn't, he wanted a quick chat.

I tried to pull myself together and clung onto the door handle and focused very hard on Jim and his forthcoming question.

"So what position do you want to play in this weekend, Simon?" He asked with an intense look on his face.

"I" I said, it was a good start. "want..............to" I tried to continue. Shit! what was the question again?

"Position?" Jim reminded me. He must have been suspicious. I had nearly collapsed to the floor and was hanging on to the door for dear life, now completely unable to focus my gaze. He didn't show his obvious disappointment at my inability to stay sober the night before my big Jets debut, but he was annoyed.

"Meedawl" I heard myself say, confirming my desire to play in the middle blocking position.

"OK! get a good nights sleep then." He muttered and then thank god, he left.

I was now collapsed to one knee and trying to locate my room key. I finally found it in my pocket and then began the Mission Impossible attempt to get the key in the hole. I managed it after what seemed like hours and stumbled through the door and into the room. It was time to test whether I was pissed or not. Once again the tell tale signs of not being able to talk, see or walk had still not convinced me that I was inebriated. With no book available I was forced to try my back up system, could I watch and see what was on television. I began my search for the T.V, there wasn't one. I laid onto the bed and looked up to see the T.V on a bracket high up on the wall.

With a huge effort I stood up and began to fumble with the controls, the T.V sparked into life. I returned to the bed to watch and make my final decision on my level of sobriety. I looked at the T.V and the colours blurred into one. I focused harder and the next thing I knew the T.V had leapt off it's bracket and was lurching viciously back and forth across the room. Once again I surmised I was in some bother.

I drifted off to sleep and woke sharply around 5.00am. I felt so bad

Luckily I still had my clothing on so I hurried out of the door and began to try to walk off my hangover around the town. I felt more and more nauseous so I headed down towards the river Tay. I sat on the bank and I just wanted to die. Having stayed by the river for some time and unfortunately experienced an impromptu bout of vomiting, narrowly missing some ducks, I headed towards the Sport Centre. With a combination of me not being in a fit state to play and Jim Wylie refusing to give court time to an alcoholic sassanach I had no part in the tournament.

A 'depth charge' as I found out on the Sunday afternoon from the highly amused players, when my power of speech and rational thought returned, is a pint with whiskey in it. Thanks lads.

Pre-Games crisis and the final squad selection, 1990-1991. Let the Games commence............

When finally faced with the decision to move to Scotland, in September 1990, for a further years study, I found that it was not what I wanted. I decided to stay in England and launch my art business SG Art, many of you will still have one of my T-shirts in your kit draw. It was a demanding year running the business, but it gave me the time to continue playing volleyball.

I played half a season with Portsmouth in division one. The team was young and we struggled to compete effectively. My shoulder was very bad and I was unable to hit for most games. By Christmas I had stopped playing with them and my only access to volleyball was with W.S.I.H.E in the Sussex volleyball league.

My luck in volleyball had remained poor since the Perth Tournament. Portsmouth didn't go well, my shoulder got worse and a trip with my old mates up at Crewe and Alsager College to play a New Years volleyball tour in the Netherlands had come to a disastrous end.

On the way to Dover, in the team minibus, we parked up at a pub on route and had a drink. On returning to the bus we discovered it had be broken into and all our passports, coats, cameras and money had disappeared. The Crewe lads sorted themselves out back in Manchester and salvaged something from the tour. I lost any desire to play and returned home.

New Year came and went, it was now 1991 the year of the next World Student Games in Sheffield. A year I had been preparing for over the last three seasons and now I was almost back to square one. I wasn't playing division one volleyball, I was injured and I was convinced I couldn't make it through the final trials.

The final set of trials for the twelve Games spots were scheduled over a month. Three weekends of camps and the British Championships with the final Sunday trial culminating in the players not selected being told the decision at the venue, no letters this time.

I was in a slump and close to dropping out of the trials. I still can't believe I nearly gave the whole thing up. Then it all got a bit Rocky Balboa. My brother convinced me to try out and offered to drive me to the first trial. My Girlfriend Freddie, now my wife, talked me into doing two weeks of intense training before the first weekend. I worked hard on my fitness, my jump and my shoulder and went into the W.S.I.H.E gym everyday to hit some balls.

The first set of trials went well, I had defended, passed and blocked well enough to obscure my hitting problems from the coaches. The British Championships, hosted by Sheffield was a good tournament for me and I re-established myself as starting six player. The only thorn in my side was the addition of a new coach Bobby Stokes, a Scottish women's coach, who had come in to assist Keith Nicholls. Bobby did some good things for the team, but he wanted big guys playing. I wasn't big. So I was finding court time hard to come by as the coaching staff tended to favour Alex Gunn (6ft 5in) and Chris Hykiel (6ft 8in). This provided me with the impetus to fight. Our system involved the middle players passing. especially against powerful jump serves. The type of serves we would face at the Games.

The final trial camp came around and sixteen players were invited to contest the twelve places. It wasn't a pleasant experience being up against good friends for the right to fulfil each of our dreams. To be fair, under pressure, everyone played very well and it must have been hard for the coaches to make their decisions. Every block was precious, every big hit was a boost, every pass had to be nearly perfect, every serve tough and each defensive ball had to chased. It was definitely the right atmosphere within which to develop the eventual tournament players.

Small moments stood out and I clearly remember making a defensive dig at the expense of another player. I was on court with Nigel Stockhill in a defensive drill where two players shared a half court each you set up first to defend cross court and then line, with the hitters choosing how the attacked. One of the hitters on Nigel's line got a tight set, he moved forward expecting a tip ball, but the ball was poked over his head to the baseline. I was completely in the zone in that drill and as Nigel closed his eyes in frustration at having being caught out of position I set off in pursuit of the ball which was dropping in the far corner to me. I got close to where the ball was going to land and hours of diving over ropes with Sava came back to me. I launched myself at the ball and made a one handed diving pick-up just before the ball hit the floor. The ball found Nigel who had turned round to see why the players surrounding the court were clapping and shouting. I remember the look of resignation on his face as he realised I had probably just done myself a big favour and all he could contribute was to dig the ball back over the net. That play steeled me and if there was a defining moment for me from that camp, it was that which sealed my place.

The Sunday came and we made our way from a hotel in Sheffield to a prison sports hall in Hull. It was a great facility but a depressing and inappropriate venue for the last trial day. We all played hard again and finished with some games.

The session was over and the coaches sat and deliberated. They were at the far end of the sports hall and we, having showered and changed to head off home were at the other end. The coaches headed over to us and asked us all to leave the hall, as we walked out they moved amongst and tapped players on the shoulder. It was like a dance contest where the judges tap your shoulder to let you know you are out. Twelve players assembled outside the gym, we went around and congratulated each other at getting in, a mixture of joy and relief, but it was still strangely subdued. We waited for athletes not selected to come out of the hall, we had no choice seeing as we were locked in the prison compound.

I looked around to take in who had made it along with myself. In the middle Chris Hykiel, Alex Gunn, Mike Boxwell and Andy Marshall. The setters were Neil Withington and Steve Milne. Outside players were the legendary Mike Rhodes and Roger Hunter (probably our best players), Craig Torrance, Nigel Gallaway and Mark Arme.

The non-selected players stepped out into the sun, after an hour of debriefing and questioning. All four players were my friends, Calvin Morriss and Nigel Stockill from Crewe and Alsager College, were good friends. They stood a moment, with James Alsopp and Pepe Diassio, adjusting to the light. Players got up from the grass and walked over to them to shake hands and commiserate. The whole thing felt really shit at that moment, although the relief of selection and not having to face the long journey home in abject depression, didn't subside.

Several years later, when it was appropriate, I talked to Calvin and Nigel about what they did on the way back from the trials that day. Nigel admitted that they gave the car keys to Mark Arme and told him to drive. They travelled five miles in silence and then asked Mark to pull over next to a shop. They went into the shop and brought twenty fags and a large bottle of scotch. Over the next two hours they consumed the lot and through copious and disgusting abuse of the coaches who had ditched them, they managed to alleviate some of the pain.

For the rest of us we had days for the decision to sink in and then a month of training and preparation for the Games. It was an incredible time, safe in the knowledge that we were in the team, we had four weeks to get in the best shape we could to take on the some of the World's best.

The final twelve were never going to set the world alight, but we were playing some pretty good volleyball and were beginning to work as a solid unit. Mike Rhodes and Roger Hunter gave us stability out wide, Neil Withington was a good setter, Steve Milne a talented opposite player and Alex Gunn a developing middle blocker. Players like Chris Hykiel, Mark Arme and Andy Marshall provided solid support from the bench.

Neil, Chris, Craig and I were over the moon. We had started the build up to Sheffield as original members of the Students team that played in the British Championships in Weston Super Mare, 1989. We racked up about twenty nine caps each, over the three years and we had become good friends. Neil's value to the squad was his accurate setting ability and his dependable nature. He was fantastically even tempered, but at the same time he was undoubtedly a hard man, the sort of bloke you wanted to be on court with when the going got tough. I only ever saw Neil lose his temper once in five years of playing volleyball on the same teams as him. It reinforced the generally held opinion that Neil could look after himself.

We were at the Fosters tournament in Poole, summer 1989. It was one of those days when we couldn't win a game for love nor money. We were in the last game of the day and had just suffered the indignity of a 15-0 drubbing in set one, at the hands of Wessex, fielding the likes of Anthony Roberts, Chris Eaton, Paul Curtis, Rob Smith and Andy Cranstone. There were a number of spectators and it was a humiliating scoreline. In set two we carried on in the same vein. Neil was experiencing the thing that setters hate most, the passers in his team were spraying the ball all over the court, he could barely touch the passes let alone set them with any effect.

At 11-3 down in set two I shanked a pass towards the scorer's table and the second referee stood at the far net post, Neil chased off after the pass and came face to face with his nemesis. Neil only ever hated one man in volleyball and Paul Edwards of Speedwell was that man, he was also the second referee. Paul could be the most infuriating player I have ever played against. He wasn't a particularly good volleyball player, but he got court time because he was always able to illicit several points and a sprinkling of red and yellow cards from opposition players due of his unsurpassed ability to wind you up. Paul stood his ground and Neil pulled up in his chase for the errant ball, a ball that he definitely would have played if the Paul hadn't been in his way, smiling his nasty little smile.

Neil still trying to compete in the game went to the first referee and pointed out that he couldn't get to play the ball because of the second ref.

The first referee, keen to get the game over, and get out on the beers, patronisingly waved Neil's protest away. Neil returned moodily to his place on court and as he prepared to play the next point Paul Edwards, still supposedly officiating the game, spoke to Neil, quite clearly and audibly.

"You don't wanna complain about stuff like that mate, you wanna teach your useless team to pass properly." He snarled in his broad west country accent. It was a fair point, but in the context of this game it was not appreciated by Neil.

Neil stopped the next server with a wave of his hand and walked slowly over to me, with no sign of malice in his face he quietly spoke.

"Shank the next pass you get in the direction of the second official." He said, I wasn't about to argue.

I got served on the next point. I did exactly as Neil asked and the pass floated in the same arc as the previous point which Neil had chased. I was completely unaware of Neil's intentions, but looked on amazed and delighted as Neil set off in pursuit of the ball. With absolutely no attempt to play the ball Neil sprinted straight at the second official, I suddenly cottoned on.

Neil absolutely creamed him and Paul went flying. Capital City exited the tournament, with Neil smiling angelically. That was it, I never saw him really angry again.

As a squad the students gained confidence for the 'big one' from some good results in various events, including two 3-2 losses to both the Latvian and Lithuanian National teams at the Pan European tournament in Oxford.

Off the court we had an almost even split of Scots and English. This lead to post training Scotland versus England five-a-side soccer games and back at the hotel some evil international bouts of Trivial Pursuit. All of which helped to bond the team. By the time the Games arrived we had formed into a pretty tight unit on and off court.

What really made the team tick was the influence of one player, our Captain Mike Rhodes. There are characters everywhere in volleyball. Some popular and funny, some aggressive and difficult and some a big pain in the arse, but all characters adding colour and life to our volleyball experiences.

Mike Rhodes was a player who commanded tremendous respect and loyalty from everyone he played with. In addition to his solid and dependable personal qualities he was generally acknowledged, by my generation, as the clown prince of volleyball, one of the funniest men I have ever met.

Michael was a short player, only six feet, but a giant character and a really talented swing hitter. I have seen him play some games of genius for Scotland and Kilmarnock and admired his qualities both as a player and Captain, but most of all he has on many occasions reduced me to tears of laughter recounting stories or just by having court side seats at the 'Mikey' show.

I was talking recently with a group of players about characters in the game and out of the six or so players in the group, three named Mike Rhodes in their lists. All three told me a Rhodez story that even I, as a collector of Mike Rhodes memorabilia, had not heard.

They were on a training camp with Mike and the team had all headed out to an Old Orleans restaurant. Their waitress came to the table and introduced herself, Mike smiled at her and very carefully asked her to bring 'two pitchers' of water to the table. The waitress, probably feeling that he was getting into the U.S spirit with his 'pitchers' comment, left to fetch the water and the players just thought it was a Mike type phrase.

The waitress returned and Mike was ready, as she walked up the table a 'pitcher' in each hand he said "Hmm? nice jugs!". Mike had obviously been planning that for some time, maybe years, and the fact that he finally got to deliver the line started him laughing. He has an infectious laugh and on this occasion nearly rendered himself unconscious while giggling. The waitress was laughing so hard she dropped one of the 'pitchers' and needless to say the tale has become volley-legend.

During the three years that he was in the squad he was always able to keep us entertained on journeys and in boring hotel foyers with a string of descriptions of various things that had happened to him in the weeks between training camps.

Most of Mike's tales included the consumption of alcohol leading to something funny happening. He once recounted a domestic stand off that he and his Father were having, with regard to Mikes nocturnal habits, his insistence on returning via a long muddy ditch on the way back home from the pub and upsetting their terrier dog at all hours of the night. His Father had issued an ultimatum, one more disturbed nights sleep due to Mike's antics and his Father would throw him out.

With this in mind he went out for some beers a few days later and although he admitted he had probably had too many, he was very controlled on the way home and declined the walk back through the muddy ditch, favouring the pavement instead.

On returning to his house he unlocked the door quietly and patted the dog carefully so it hardly made a noise. He went upstairs to bed and as his head hit the pillow he thought how well he had done to miss the ditch, not be sick and keep the dog quiet and drifted off into a fitful sleep.

His next memory was his Father gently waking him and asking if he was all right. Mike said he was and continued weeing. Unfortunately he was weeing in his Mother's wardrobe into which he had sleep walked just minutes earlier. Mike lived with a friend for a few weeks after that.

Mike could never do anything in a straightforward manner. In 1993, after the Games, I was staying with my parents before moving into my new house with my girlfriend. They owned a small Post Office in a village called Hamble, just outside Southampton. Mike on his way through from Scotland to a holiday in Cornwall, had decided to pay me a visit, unannounced. I was at work and my parents were in the shop, Mike came in posing as an Italian pro-volleyball scout and in front of a shop full of customers asked my Mum if the Italian volleyball club 'Stacksio Doshio' could purchase her son for the forthcoming season. Mum and the customers were in stitches as Mike, in a long coat a baseball cap and a huge false moustache wrote out a Royal Bank of Scotland cheque for one hundred million Lire, then left.

Mike is a generous, kind and thoughtful man, but he was always one for scrapes or simply engineering improbable 'Pythonesque' situations from which he and others could derive incredible amusement. Most sound implausible at best and maybe to those of you hearing them second hand, unfunny. But if you were there.....

I roomed with Mike and Neil at the World Student Games and each night something would happen.

The nights and the entertainment rolled on. Mike returned late one night with Steve Milne, another Scottish player. They switched on the lights in the flat and informed me that they were going to play 'Hollywood celebrity death scene' and I could watch or join in. I decided to watch.

The game, which I had never seen before and have not seen since, was pretty straight forward. I was elected the judge and had to score each competitor out of ten for their performance. The contestant had a five minute time slot to stage the most elaborate Hollywood 'Oh no! I've been shot', death scene.

Even though this was the first time they had competed the standard was high. Mike of course edged it with a touching death scene that lead him, after being shot, first to take a piss in the loo while moaning loudly, then die over the whole room, plus bunk beds. Eventually coming to what appeared to be the bitter end by rolling slowly away under the bottom bunk, only to fart and revive himself for another minute of staggering. Not a dry eye in the house, quiet literally.

A few nights later, Mike and I were wandering back from the bar and Mike spotted a male games athlete, with a female games athlete, both foreign competitors. He suggested we follow them, we did. We followed them for miles through the tower block accommodation carefully hiding as they stopped to snog at various places. They finally came to rest on the front of a soft drinks retail machine and were so engrossed in their foreplay that we got to the far side of the machine unnoticed. I had no idea where all this was going, but Mike had obviously hatched a plan some time ago. As the couple reached what could be described as the heat of passion Mike leapt out from behind the machine and shouted in a broad Glaswegian accent, "leave my fucking sister alone!".

The male athlete was shocked it would be fair to say, but he quickly recovered his composure as he realised his hot date was now a dead weight, she had fainted. We, Mike, me and the male athlete (who spoke no English) dragged her back towards his apartment. She was now conscious and mumbling. Mine and Mike's giggling however, soon turned to yet more tears of hysterical laughter as we watched the dejected sexually frustrated male athlete drag his date by both legs along the polished corridor to be met by her room mates who immediately began to interrogate him. "She's all yours mate." Said Mike, and we ran off.

With Mike at the helm we were a good team and with the Games now ready to begin our motivation was unquestionable.

The World Student Games, 1991.
The final reckoning.....

The final information pack arrived for the volleyball team, giving us details of where to meet and at what time. The whole British World Student Games team was scheduled to arrive in Sheffield, on the afternoon of July 14th 1991. By the time I got to the large council offices, doubling as the accreditation facilities, there were hundreds of athletes from many different disciplines milling around and queuing for passes. I said my goodbyes to girlfriend, brother and parents and they headed off to stay locally with relatives and to watch the first volleyball match of the event, Great Britain versus Germany, to be played at the end of week one.

Each athlete filled through and showed their letter of invitation to the Games and valid I.D, with that checked you were handed a stamped photo accreditation pass, indicating the competition you were in and the Games venues you could visit. Your pass was a major key, it got you food, drinks, accommodation and entry into a range of sporting events.

Having got my pass I wore it proudly, despite thousands of other athletes who also got a pass I was wearing mine like I was the only person who got one. I wandered through the building to the designated volleyball meeting spot and met up with the majority of the team, completely beside ourselves with utter excitement. We were there, we had made it and in just a couple of hours we would be in to the Games village. We headed off to the village, a completely re-furbished tower block in the heart of Sheffield, right next to the brand new International sports complex Ponds Forge. The Forge is one of my favourite places to play and watch volleyball, all because of it's connection in my mind with the Games. It was to be the venue for our first three matches as the host team.

On arrival at the village gates we met our team liaison for the two weeks, Rob. Rob was a great bloke and seemed really stoked to be our chaperone. I couldn't help feeling sorry for him, he could have been assigned to any British squad, some even won medals, instead he had been given the volleyball team. Unfortunately, we were the weakest squad there apart from maybe Hong Kong. Rob never showed any disappointment at not being placed with a contender.

I mentioned the Hong Kong team because they epitomised a spirit that used to be such a wonderful part of the Olympic movement, now sadly lost to sponsors, media pressure and the spectre of the qualifying time. The Hong Kong athletes, with the exception of some archers and a gymnast, were absolutely terrible. The beauty of their entry into the Games was that they didn't give a damn about that, they were there to compete as well as they could and to learn and develop. Their women's volleyball team were so bad they lost our British women in one of the games of the tournament, with hundreds of spectators crammed into the Hillsborough stadium shouting their heads off the British team won 3-1.

The track and field events at the games were sensational with some of the worlds most talented athletes in attendance. The likes of Fiona May, Steve Backley and Geoff Parsons were competing for Great Britain. The Hong Kong athletes in track and field never made it through any rounds and they included in their number a wonderful young lady who's performance in the one hundred metres will live in my memory. A real 'Eric the Eel' moment. In the women's one hundred the field was almost World class, save for this one gem of a competitor from Hong Kong. We watched her heat completely by accident, on the television in the tower block common room. She came out to the track looking so serious and took up her position just back from the starting line with the other runners, she couldn't have been more than five feet tall and was sandwiched between two lycra clad six foot Amazonian wonder women from recognised sprinting nations. She had rejected lycra in favour of a white polo shirt and a baggy pair of navy blue shorts, on the shirt was scrawled HONG KONG in black felt tip.

The starter called the athletes to their marks and in a amazing act of defiance the runner from Hong Kong refused to go up to the start line, she insisted on taking an upright running start just like on school sports day, a metre and a half behind her illustrious opponents. It was a hilarious picture. The gun went and the lycra clad machines screamed off down the track, the girl from Honkers did a kind of Tom and Jerry cartoon start, taking several frantic running steps without actually moving. She was already twenty metres down by the time she left her mark, she put in an incredible and honest effort, trying to run as fast as she possibly could. At the halfway mark she opened her eyes and noticed the rest of the field had already finished and she now had centre stage. She didn't waste her opportunity and jogged the remaining fifty metres to rapturous applause from the crowd.

The only people who didn't share in the joy of that one hundred metres moment were the supercilious old farts in the commentary box, who huffily talked about qualifying standards and no place in World sport for that type of display, while their fat little pot bellies hung over their all too tight trousers and they sycophantically massaged the ego of some ageing track star who could barely string a coherent sentence together without recourse to at least twenty 'know what I means ?'

At the Games village, Rob our liaison, showed us up to our two flats. All the teams were roomed in two or three flats depending on the size of the squad. We fitted in to two flats and the coaching staff in to another. Each flat was basic, but modern and newly decorated, with two sleeping areas and a toilet and shower. I roomed with Mike Rhodes and Neil Withington and Mike Boxwell, Steve Milne and Alex Gunn occupied the other bedroom. After settling in we set off to explore and arranged to meet at the dining hall, as a team, for our first evening meal.

The village was huge. The complex housed seven tower blocks, six sleeping the athletes, coaches and physios and one acting as the administration nerve centre for the games. At low level, the former parade of shops had been converted into, more shops. There were sports shops, gift shops, the official Games office, a Post Office, cafes and a small supermarket and then a large two storey pub come night-club. Outside the parade of shops was a tastefully arranged piazza with chairs, tables and umbrellas. The effect was excellent, the athletes could be completely self-sufficient, which considering the backlash from local residents over the cost of the Games being added to their ever increasing council tax was probably not a bad thing.

Most athletes chose to remain within the giant compound, there was so much to do there. Only the Kenyan long distance runners decided to venture beyond the confines of the village and the adjacent Don Valley athletics stadium . The Kenyans found a great piece of long flat road that they could jog on for miles, we like to call it the M1 and the police, who arrested fourteen African men racing along the hard shoulder, called it an offence. Some nifty diplomatic work had to done to sort out that misunderstanding.

The dining hall was part of a massive tented area , bigger than any food hall I have ever seen. It was my favourite place in the village for two reasons, firstly the fantastic choice of food all available in large never ending quantities to satisfy even the big athletes. Secondly, it was the village meeting place, where as time went on, you could dine alongside sports people from many different disciplines, countries, religions and racial backgrounds. It was a very friendly place to be and provided us with some amazing memories.

The two things that really stood out from the two weeks of three meals a day, were the Chinese gymnastic squad and the massed South Korean track and field team. The Chinese gymnasts were a ludicrous example of the way that so many countries flaunt clear International sports rules. To play in the Games you had to be over sixteen and under twenty seven. The gymnasts were tiny, scared little girls. True, they had more International competitive experience in their little fingers than the whole of the British volleyball squad, but they looked to be between eight and twelve years old. They were fascinated by the atmosphere in the tented hall, but they were shy and timid. Their size and fragility was even more shockingly emphasised because of the chaperone chosen to accompany them to meals. She was seven foot tall, seriously she was a seven foot, Chinese basketball player. She wasn't, as you would expect of a person of that height, skinny. She was actually built like a shot putter. Every night she and ten little pixies would come in for their meal. They would chatter away to her and she would crane her head down to hear what they were saying, every so often they would swing on her or climb around her frame while she stood in the queue like a giant oak tree.

Having seen my own young female cousins reject plates of food at the same age as the Chinese gymnasts, in favour of a single slice of Marmite on toast and seen them push already minuscule servings of food around their plate, the quantities of food the little gymnasts ate was astonishing. They would each carry three loads of food back to the table. Noodles, rice, fruit and a plate of meat. They would stack it up and the basketball player would watch over them as they ate it, all of it. We would often leave the hall as it was shutting for the day and pass a table of tiny gymnasts looking fed-up and full-up, but still with bowls rice to consume, they didn't leave until it was gone.

The South Koreans were another story all together. They would come to dinner in their brightly coloured, garish tracksuits and stand chatting in the queue. They would always smile and nod at you, but when you spoke to them they had no English and we certainly had no Korean. The Western revolution that hit Japan in the eighties and is now creeping into Chinese life, was permeating Korean teen culture in 1991. They were all sporting big, new romantic hairstyles, groovy sneakers and shades. There was always music playing in the main tent, something to listen to when queuing for food. The Koreans

73

would ignore most of it and continue chatting and laughing. Then, when one tune and one tune only came on, M.C Hammer and 'Hammertime', they would all spontaneously break into jerky awkward dance moves. They looked like a scene from fame when the arty farty students just can't control themselves any longer and they jus' gotta' dance man.

We loved it and the Koreans pretty soon learned they had an audience, the caterers on seeing them enter the tent, would deliberately rig the P.A system to play the song. It was genius, they would all jerk back and forth with their version of Asian body-popping and then at the chorus they would shout, as one, the only English word they had managed to figure out from the whole track.

"HAMMER TIME!" They all screamed in unison with huge toothy grins and heavy Korean accents, the tent used to go berserk.

We trained in Ponds Forge the next morning, training went well and spirits were understandably high, too high for my liking. Towards the end of the session the P.A system boomed into life and announced that there was an urgent phone call for Mr Simon Golding. Already harbouring thoughts of television commentary fame I found it completely normal that I would be called at a major sporting venue in such a way. I left the session and went up to reception, where three confused receptionists told me they had never heard of me and knew absolutely nothing about a message for me. I returned to the arena, still not suspicious of the incident. When I got back in to the main hall it was completely deserted, balls, ball wagons, kit bags, coaches and athletes all gone. I suddenly knew I had been stitched. Like all of us do I had to go along with things, trying to get the right balance between 'yeh! you certainly got me' (which they had) and how long you wandered around looking like a jerk in front of your peers. They let me suffer for sometime, I gave up looking for them and quietly packed my bag to leave, maybe they had gone already and I was stood in vast hall talking to myself. I walked slowly across the floor towards the exit and as I did so the P.A spoke once more.

"Phone call for Mr Golding." Said a familiar voice.

I turned around to find the whole team stood up from various hiding places and Mike Boxwell on the commentary microphone doing his best northern female receptionist impression. Bastards!

That evening Mike Rhodes decided to entertain the team with his legendary bad magic show. Mike had planned to put on an incredible trick for all of us, once again the act in itself was funny enough. The punch line was, that he would take Neil Withington's contact lenses (our only setter, his only pair of contacts) as his prop for the trick. The planned hilarious conclusion was to pretend to slip and throw the lenses out of the window, the window of course would be closed. We were staying on about the fourteenth floor of a large tower block in the games village, all went according to plan and Mike tripped and launched himself at the window aiming to tip the contents onto the glass, but cause Neil to think the worst.

When you have had a couple of beers, mere detail becomes a secondary consideration and the mere detail that someone had opened the window was overlooked by the 'Great Stupendo' Rhodes. So with a convincing comedy trip Mike launched the lenses towards and out of the tower block window. We liked it a lot, we clapped and laughed, Neil didn't like it, the first game was only days away. Neil went white and Mike improvised with a show stopping mime grope for a non-existent window pane before collapsing on the floor in uncontrollable laughter. Neil visited the opticians the next day.

The Opening Ceremony, corporate gaffs and the first game..............

Day two was looking like another exciting day in international sports paradise, with training in the early afternoon and then in the evening we were to attend the event we had been most looking forward to, besides the first game, the opening ceremony.

Time for departure to the ceremony arrived and athletes were loaded onto scores of coaches to head to Don Valley stadium where a sell out twenty five thousand crowd were in attendance, the crowd included many of our friends and relatives. The journey down to the stadium revealed a side to the Sheffield people that we had been completely unaware of. We had been encouraged to stay within the compound of the village and force fed a diet of media rhetoric about the feelings of the disaffected city residents now facing an increased council tax to pay for the Games folly. We believed that we were most unwelcome guests. On the journey down the Sheffield hills through the streets of terraced housing which was home to the very people who were going to suffer most from an increase in rates, we were treated like kings. Not one bad word was shouted, not one object thrown to break a coach window, just rows and rows of people all waving Union Jacks and cheering and clapping. Away from the grassroots support for the team and driving through the industrial section of the City we did eventually encounter a small group of protesters directing vitriolic abuse to the athletes, but that was all we saw.

We arrived at Don Valley and Games officials organised us into rows ready to march into the stadium. The British team were to be last in. Each team had been instructed to walk one lap of the stadium's four hundred metre track and then take their designated place on the field in the centre of the arena. From our position outside we could see lights, fireworks and hear absolutely deafening cheers from the crowd. We stood outside for nearly an hour, but rather than getting bored it was just like queuing for a big ride at a theme park with the anticipation and excitement simply being heightened by the wait.

We were stood in amongst hundreds of British athletes, some would go on to even higher honours and experience this spine tingling moment, but on a bigger stage at the Olympic Games. For many of us it would be the only time that we would walk out in front of thousands of people at a major sporting event. Despite all your hopes and dreams for your future many of us knew that this was going to be our only chance at a moment like this and we were going to make the most of it.

The officials issued us with little Union Jack flags on sticks and bags of sweeties to throw to the kids in the crowd. We were given the nod to enter the stadium, all of us following Steve Backley who had been selected to carry the flag. The other team members and myself filed towards the stadium entrance, a huge set of doors which swung apart to reveal a walkway into the arena. I can still see the picture in my head and just writing this piece, the hairs on the back of my neck are standing up, exactly as they did that night. At the point the players drew level with the entrance they all went silent and began to register the sight that awaited us. I went silent because I wanted to clear my head and take in everything that was about to happen, I wanted to experience and hopefully remember every part of the ceremony.

We walked through the doors and the noise hit us, it was a thunderous mass to begin with and then as your mind adjusted you could start to pick out individual shouts and the mass chanting of 'GB! GB!' We began to realise it was all for us, the athletes from all the other nations were clapping and waving and twenty five thousand people were directing their sole attentions towards the British team. The stadium seemed huge, the floodlights filled the space with an amazing light as they rose high around the perimeter of the stadium like a scene from 'Close Encounters.'

Once you were in the moment took over. We all stayed in ranks talking and comparing our feelings with those around us and trying to process the many pieces of unfamiliar information that were bombarding our senses. The effect was exquisite, a heaving mass of varied colour not a single gap in the seating which was totally packed. From the track, waving our flags it was a complete being, a functioning, breathing, chanting form. When you ventured beyond the track with your sweeties it separated out into individuals all shouting for the team, smiling, laughing, leaning over the barriers to shake hands with you. Twenty four thousand nine hundred and ninety two of them I didn't know me from Adam, but their enthusiasm and their genuine affection for you as a team member was truly humbling. It was an incredibly inspiring moment for the athletes and in that ten minutes that it took to walk round the track we were completely rewarded for persevering with the student programme.

We all wanted to do another circuit, the crowd noise had not abated, they were shouting for more. Officials weren't having any of it and ushered us into our designated spot on the field, the Games had to go on. We all stood in rows and let the moment sink in awaiting the next elements of the ceremony.

The stadium commentator let us know that the female astronaut Helen Sharp was now entering the stadium with the World Student Games flame, burning brightly on top of a torch. We watched proudly as the flame made it's way down the home straight and towards the hill at the far end of the stadium where the event flame was to be lit. The flame suddenly disappeared from view. The astronaught had tripped over her own feet and in front of twenty five thousand people had fallen arse over tit, spilling the flame in small pieces of still burning rag all over the track. Officials picked her up and scooped burning embers back into the torch end. With a now barely alight flame she staggered off, clearly injured, but determined to finish the job. She wobbled a few times but made it to the top of the hill. We hoped that even though she was an athlete she was also a smoker so she could use her lighter to spark the event flame, because the torch she was carrying didn't look like it would do the job. Miraculously the flame of hope for young athletes World-wide burst into flickering life along with lights sweeping the stadium and an awesome firework display, the Games were on.

We all returned to the village, buzzing with the tremendous excitement of the whole evenings events, proud to the core to be part of the team and feeling like we were really part of the whole rich Games pageant.

The following day was another morning training session, this time with no spoof phone calls. After the session the whole squad joined the entire British team for a corporate afternoon lunch with the businesses that had contributed financially to staging the Games. The afternoon had the local dignitaries scrabbling to attend with the promise of a formal meeting with the Princess Ann. On arrival at the 'do' each team had a squad photograph taken as a memento of the Games, then they were taken to an area of the tented corporate village to eat and await their audience with the Princess. We were all pretty excited about meeting Royalty and had also been told that we would be introduced to a few hundred big players from the British business community. It was a bit like being a zoo exhibit, to be honest. Each team was placed in a small annexe within the tents, we were asked to remain within these areas leaving only to procure food from an excellent buffet in the main tent.

We stuffed ourselves full of delicious food, not a rissole in sight, and had a few glasses of champagne, by 2.00pm we were ready to meet business people and Royalty. We would be ready for a long time as it turned out. We stood at what appeared to be the end of a very long queue of teams waiting to meet the dignitaries. It soon became obvious that meeting the volleyball team was at the bottom of everyone's, including the Princess's, list. The main attraction for the guests, after meeting Steve Backley that is, was meeting the enormous GB Men's Basketball team. Most of the players were big, six foot plus, but some were huge, six foot ten and built like WWF wrestlers. I had gone down to dinner the day before and got into a lift with three of the basketball players, all stooping to fit in. They filled the eight person lift so that I had to squeeze in to the tiny space that remained.

The businessmen didn't really talk much with anyone except themselves, indicative of society as a whole the majority of the corporate moguls were men. Balding, overweight, big cigars and loud, all the stereotypes you could conjure up were there. The other stereotype clearly visible to a dedicated people watcher like myself were their much younger, generally glamorous, fashion conscious wives. These wives were very keen on meeting the athletes, one group in particular, the male basketball players. The volleyball team, now a couple of hours past our best, stood (there were no chairs to sit on) and watched fascinated and maybe jealous as hoards of women flocked around the basketball team. They all wanted photo's taken with the really big players and as they lined up they were all chatting with each other, raising eyebrows and making lewd comments about various parts of the athlete's collective anatomy's. There was a lot of giggling and ogling, occasionally one of the players would bend down and make a charming comment to a group of women, adding to the frisson of the moment. Great guffaws of laughter broke out as one of the players told a large gang of flirtatious groupies "You know what they say, big feet..................big shoes."

We gradually realised that no corporate delegates were going to pay us a visit, much less the Princess Royal, players began to drop like flies, the champagne, rich food and no toilet were taking their toll. We laid around as a group, it didn't make for a pretty picture, but we had been stood for nearly four hours and hadn't been visited by even an ugly myopic corporate wife mistaking us for bone fide sportsmen. As usual with groups of disaffected twenty something lads we began to chat and of course to mess about. During one particularly silly moment as players were telling jokes and making humorous comments about corporate wives and well hung basketball players, we got the giggles and began to lose what remained of our inhibitions. I can't remember for the life of me who did it, but one player began to do his impression of how he would behave in the presence of a corporate wife mob.

He put on a lounge lizard voice and slimy look and began to make double entendre suggestions with a solicitous raising of one eyebrow, Roger Moore style. He had us in stitches, especially when he began to discuss his physical attributes with the excited bunch of made up groupies. "I'm a volleyball player madam, I'm hung like a pony.................a Shetland pony!"

That was it we really got the giggles, silly boy's disease my Mum used to call it. The giggles not unpredictably were suddenly interrupted by a volley of farts, food and champagne induced. I joined the party with my own offering, it was an absolute shocker and the team quite rightly laid into to me while bemoaning the hideous smell. We were shaken from a reverie by a small man looking down at our group with a clearly visible expression of disdain. Princess Anne's equerry told us that the Princess was now ready to meet us. We leapt up and tried to restore some order while fanning away furiously with our corporate programmes trying to move the smell from our airless corner of the tent. We were the last team that she met, but she spent time with us talking to and shaking hands with all the players and making us feel like we were part of the whole Games experience again.

With only two days to go before we met Germany in the first game, the tension and excitement was increasing. The other phenomena now present was the time honoured paranoia about which players would get the starting six positions for game one. We had a good idea of what the starting six positions would be, over the last year the squad had settled down to a relatively established six. I was usually in that six, but my confidence in a starting place had been dented by the arrival of Bobby Stokes as Keith Nicholls coaching assistant. Bobby wanted to play the bigger middle blockers, at six foot two I was easily the smallest middle player at the tournament, most of the middle blockers were six foot four plus. It didn't matter to Bobby what I could bring to the team as a passer, defender and improving sideout hitter, we all knew I had little or no chance to form an effective and consistent block at the net.

During training I concentrated hard on making blocks and had some success, but I was still unsure of what decision the coaches would make, especially in light of the German line up. The Germans, now a unified Nation, could field the cream of their volleyball talent. Most of their players were students, so in effect the German student side were their World League National squad and one of the hot favourites to make the Final. They included players like Dornheim the setter and huge hitters Stutzke and six foot eleven Kleinbub. The game was going to be difficult.

We had a training match organised against Belgium in a sport centre outside Sheffield, we trekked off to the game on a bus. The players and coaches were beginning to focus on the German game, the training match was the last chance for us to prove we were worth a starting six place. The atmosphere on the bus was in stark contrast to the previous months excited, relaxed and up beat behaviour. The game itself was almost a non-event, both teams switched their line-ups regularly. I played one and a half sets and then sat out the rest of the game watching the other middle blockers. We held our own against Belgium and played four scrimmage sets, all of which we lost narrowly. On the way back to the Games village the anxiety about the impending first match was highlighted by a short sharp row between Keith Nicholls the head coach and Bobby Stokes the assistant. We couldn't completely hear what it was about and it only lasted a few seconds, but whatever one of them had said was reacted to quiet sharply by the other. The atmosphere on the bus became even more subdued. Back at the village we were under strict instructions to go straight to bed after our evening meal, to get some sleep before the big game. That night, while Mike was out of the room cleaning his teeth, Neil reminded me of a pledge we had made weeks earlier. If we both made the starting six and we were both in front court, it didn't matter how bad the first pass was he was going to set the first attack to me, even if he was sliding under the scorer's table on his arse. I wanted to talk about the game, but Neil demonstrated his miraculous falling asleep within seconds trick, something he had perfected over the years. With Neil snoring loudly Mike and I chatted for a while about the Germans and our team, before we too joined Neil in the land of nod.

We awoke the next morning with a very definite feeling that the stakes had just been raised, the reason we were all here in Sheffield was finally going to happen. Our first game was just twelve hours away.

We followed the routine we had established some weeks out from the Games, trying to keep everything as close to normal as we could. Breakfast, team talk, training, good lunch, sleep in the afternoon and light food about four hours out from the game. The day passed without incident, no body got the nod with regard to places and the team talks were generic with all players issued equally with instructions, so no clues there. The time came to make our way down to Ponds Forge and although it was only a five minute walk, security dictated that we take a team coach down to the arena. We arrived and checked in at reception, from there we were taken to a preparation and warm-up area, where coaches and physios awaited our arrival. Warm-up! who needed a warm-up? all of us were right on the edge, tight because the game was nearly upon us, anxious because we still didn't know the starting six players and desperate to get out in front of the crowd and hit some balls.

The previous game finished and we were lead down to court side. The team was given the nod by an official with a headset and Walkie Talkie and we burst out from behind the curtains and ran on the brightly coloured Taraflex floor bathed in the arena lights like rugby players sprinting out on to some hallowed turf. Unfortunately the crowd, tired, hungry and thirsty after the previous game, had all buggered off for refreshments and to stretch legs. We ran out in our proudest moment to absolute bloody silence. We came down from our initial giddy mental heights and formed an embarrassed group in the centre of the floor, we looked over to the relaxed, confident Germans all laughing and chatting with each other. I had learned my lesson well from York 1986 and the stark realities of trying to pull off shock victories against quality teams. This was however 'our house' and we were all damned if we weren't going to give it a really good go, those of us that were going to be on court that is.

I warmed up with Craig Torrance, usually an infuriating player to warm-up with. He was strictly a one tap smash one hammer warm-up man. His first hit would go somewhere near you to play, the second would bounce high off the floor a good few metres away, serving no warm-up function other than to crane your neck up to the ball as it floated in the air. In that first warm-up however I was reduced through sheer nerves to the same tactics and our warm-up was almost non-existent with both players chasing their errant shots around the arena.

The whistle went for the warm-up over the net and we and the crowd in the rapidly filling grandstand seating were treated to master class of power hitting. German after German attacker rose majestically in the air, head and shoulders above the net and their bodies completely still they pummelled balls into the Ponds Forge floor. Each attacker landed and continued under the net into our space, staring at us and laughing at us. At least five of their shots reached the roof in Ponds Forge, I doubt whether I could kick the ball that high let alone bounce it of the floor first. We tried to respond aggressively and with Neil's pin point setting players like Chris Hykiel, Roger Hunter, Mark Arme and Alex Gunn, produced some quality hitting. The balance however, couldn't be restored. By the time the had pelted us with ferocious jump serves at the end of the warm-up we were absolutely clear about the task ahead. Now everyone desperately wanted to be out on the floor, to see how each of us would cope.

We returned to the sidelines for the final team talk and the moment when we found out the starting six. The crowd were now really shouting for us "GB! GB!" once again rang out, this time around the Ponds Forge Arena. To a man it was an incredibly uplifting experience and a moment of extreme pride, the ominous detail of the warm-up exhibition faded a little and we began to concentrate on us instead of them. Keith produced his clipboard and after four years of waiting and preparation finally got to announce a starting six in a World Student Games. He read it out aloud. Starting in position two Roger Hunter, one Neil Withington setting, six Alex Gunn, five Mike Rhodes, four Steve Milne and three Simon Golding. I was on, I was bloody well on and just about to play against one of the strongest sides in Europe and a top twenty side in the World.

We walked out on to the court, everything outside of the playing area seemed suddenly irrelevant. Keith came to each of us as we stood on court and thanked us, congratulated us and told us we could do it. He knew we couldn't, but he sounded very genuine at the time. It was an excellent piece of coaching and a gesture I shall always remember.

Mike Rhodes had lost the toss and so it was the Germans to serve, the first play agreement I had with Neil I assumed was still on. The first pass was a good one, I jumped and Neil set me the ball, just like he had promised I swung at it as hard as I could and bounced it straight off the German blocker's head and out over the sideline for a sideout, we went potty. Barbara Totterdell caught that shot on film (see photos section). The celebrations died down and Roger went back to serve, the Germans passed his serve in and Dornheim set the ball fast and wide to Kleinbub, who at six eleven was the tallest player on court and the second tallest behind a seven foot Russian. Kleinbub motored in, lined up cross court and pounded the shit out of the ball. I don't know how I got there but I did and I jumped as high as I have probably ever jumped, fired up on years of expectation. I blocked the ball back over his head for a point, we were one nil on Germany. If it could have ended there we could have gone home contented, unfortunately for us the referee insisted we play on and this is where the difference in class was exposed. With their superior height, strength, technical ability and full-time training programme the Germans were capable of lamping the ball every single time, we couldn't maintain out initial flourish. The first two sets were gone in the blinking of an eye.

Set three was our only real show of character. We were working very hard and playing so well, but the Germans were so adept at siding out that scoring points was almost impossible. Ask any player who has competed against a better team and they will confirm that siding out is not the problem, actually scoring points is. Under the old scoring system that is.

We went into set three, still fired up and trying to get a credible result in one of the sets. It was Roger Hunter who restored some pride. He just didn't care who he was playing against, he always gave it one hundred percent effort and tried and tried for every point. He came to the service line, he always had a strong, shallow and fast jump serve. When it went in it was devastating. He got five in on the trot and we went five nil ahead, an incredible lead. One we had no chance of keeping, but we fought hard. Such was our resistance that the Germans began to look interested for short periods of time. Keith was determined to give the bench a taste of the action and made substitutions, I came off and watched the back half of set three from the pig-pen.

The pig-pen is the self styled area where substitutes in volleyball can come to warm-up, although most stand in there and pass the time off day with each other. Sometimes cheering the team, but mostly slagging off the coaching staff for not playing them or abusing the player who is on court instead of them. We watched from the pig-pen in awe at the German offence, blocking was a nightmare of guessing wrong and being mislead by fake runs from attackers and a talented setter who watched and waited. If you stayed where you were he sped the ball wide, if you moved to anticipate he a put the ball in the gap you had just left. My Dad videoed the game, his edited highlights are a series of crunching spikes from every area of the net rained down on us by some superb volleyball athletes. In all honesty, notwithstanding Roger's efforts, little else happened that night. We lost 3-0.

Following the German game we had a two day break before we met Turkey. We trained, relaxed and got out to watch some other volleyball matches. The awesome play of the Germans had left it's mark, but with the prospect of two more pool games against top international opposition, spirits in the camp were still high.

Turkey were good, all professionals. We played one of our best games of the tournament against them and I recorded the best attacking stats for the team. My stats were courtesy of a strange hitting duel which developed between myself and the Turkish middle blocker opposite me on the rotation. Neil would set me and I would go for my favourite shot, across my body hitting to the space at position one that the penetrating setter had left. He found my hitting technique difficult to block, but far from getting angry he found it more and more amusing. His bench was shouting at him to block my shot, but all smiling at the same time. He responded with melodramatics every time I got the ball past him. Then he started doing the same shot back at me and chatting away in broken English after each play. "Yes! like that, no?"

We went down in each set to about eight or nine. In set three he called me to the net. "My shot now, I do, then you do." He said, pleased with his sentence.

The Turkish setter gave him a metre ball, a slower set in the middle. I waited and jumped to block. He left the floor with a grunt, indicating some extra effort. My block peak must have been two feet lower than his spike point and he absolutely clubbed the ball over my block and on to the floor behind me. "You like, yes?" he inquired. I smiled back, yes wonderful, I now knew it was all a bit of a game, not only couldn't I touch him, but the defender behind me now understood that I offered no protection whatsoever and his baby faced good looks were in jeopardy.

It was my turn now, the next ball I got I gave it everything on my jump and as I went to swing he was towering over me, hands obscuring my view of the court space. I cheated and hit exactly the same shot again, under his right armpit and down to one for the sideout. He landed looking incredulously at me. "Nooo!" he shouted and then turned to his bench to explain that we had a deal, he hit over me by a metre and then I tried the same thing thus allowing him to roof the shit out of me and I had failed to honour the deal.

The game finished, again a 3-0 loss, but it was a great game to play in.

Our next game was the one we were all waiting for, USA at Ponds Forge. The scramble for places was back on and with the added pressure for the coaches that this game was the last really competitive game of the event and all play-off games for the lower placings would be played in smaller venues with much smaller crowds. The players who had featured strongly in the opening games were enjoying themselves, other players with only a short time on court and some who hadn't even played yet, were getting a little disgruntled.

U.S.A, Tommy's hair and the shirts.............

There are so many cool things in volleyball that it would be tough to pick the coolest with real conviction. However, I would like at this point to venture a personal preference for the thing that has always done it for me, shirts. Yep, that's it...shirts.

There is nothing so session stopping as a player strolling in to the gym with a foreign national or national league shirt on. There is nothing more uplifting for a team than to receive some really great looking new kit.

I have been more than lucky over the years with regard to shirts. Apart from the odd nylon disaster in my college days and one complete stinker of a kit at Capital City, orange and white cheque nylon long sleeve shirt and black lycra cycling shorts, I have generally liked my kits.

On the beach my sponsorships have always been surfwear based. In 1996 and 1997 Steve Draper and I hooked up with a small off the wall company called Wookie. The company had some great stuff and when we applied our 'Timex' watches sponsorship patches to the shirts and shorts, the image was complete. In 1998 and 1999 Clayton Lucas and I were lucky enough to get a good deal with 'Kangaroo Poo', this gear on and off court was awesome and put the icing on two really superb competitive seasons.

International shirts is where the Kudos really is though. A good international shirt looks the business at training and in warm-ups. Anthony Roberts, Great Britain and Malory player, has a French national shirt which he wears now and again, it stands out a mile I have often coveted it from afar. Dave King, former England and Malory player used to pose round in a Brazil shirt at summer tournaments. I often dreamed of going up to block Dave, punching his lights out as he went to hit and then sneaking away from the ensuing melee to rifle through his bag and nick the Brazillian shirt. Marcus Russell, Steve Fee, Morph Bowes and Matt Jones, the current crop of European professional players are able to pull out a fine array of Belgian and French national league shirts that really cut the mustard.

Aside from losing three sets to nil to everyone we played in Sheffield, the overriding theme was to collect a shed load of international shirts. Getting them was really difficult though. Nobody wanted our playing shirts, apart from us who would ? So I designed a Great Britain T-shirt with a union jack sewn on to give that genuine souvenir effect. We would take these shirts and just trawl off around the games village trying to find volleyball teams who would swap.

Competition began to hot up for top shirt acquisitions and in the last week of the Games Chris Hykiel and I were going head to head for clobber. We managed to locate the South Koreans, they had bags full of kit. We went into their team flat and began to do deals. I came away with four playing shirts and two delegates shirts. The final kit haul was pretty impressive. In my collection were shirts from Turkey, Indonesia and South Korea. I was pleased with every deal except one.

I was wandering back from lunch with some washed kit, including a tracksuit, under my arm. A big Russian, at least six eight, came over to me and used the international code word for a kit exchange.

"Trade? Trade?" he asked, smiling and pointing at my tracksuit.

My tracksuit was going to be a key trading implement and we were anticipating an absolute trade-fest at the closing ceremony, with athletes stripping off left right and centre, frantically swapping kit. I anticipated being stood in Don Valley stadium in my pants, arms laden with top international kit.

On the other hand however, with regard to the big Russian, this was my opportunity to put one over on Chris and return to our accommodation with some Soviet kit casually draped over my shoulder. In truth I should have learned my lesson, I had been burned before in a most unsatisfactory eastern European kit swap with Tatra Prague and their fantastic disintegrating shirts.

My judgement temporarily clouded I decided to trade. I took my tracksuit out of it's bag and he pulled out a velour, light blue 'thing'. It was clearly the tracksuit of an even bigger bloke than him and looked like a catalogue garment that Pat from Eastenders would do the housework in, if she was six foot ten that is. It was the work of a fashion design criminal genius. I was about to refuse the swap, but he looked so pathetic and so massive, stood there with his offering. Just as I began to look suspicious about the deal he sensed my possible withdrawal and panicked, grabbing my garment he dropped his own next to me and then ran off. Confident of getting away with his crime mainly because there is only one barber in Russia and consequently the whole team had the same haircut and looked almost identical. Tall and ugly with Fray Bentos tin fringes.

The kit picture was still far from complete. In my fifteen years of playing there was one kit that stood out from all the rest. It was a design great, a kit that gave it's wearers the most sophisticated and solid team look that I have ever seen. Like any desirable work of art, it's manufacturers limited the availability, thus surrounding the product with an aura of mystique.

The 1984 and 1988 U.S.A kits were the best I have ever seen. The short sleeve, collared shirts and tailored shorts were in a class all of their own. I tried to recreate the look for the 1990 'Ambassador' shirts and the polo shirt became an instant playing choice in Britain soon after that. Now in Sheffield we were due to play the U.S.A and their wonderful, exact replica of the 1988 model, shirts.

We lost to the States three nil, but we competed well. They were very strong and their starting six had Tommy Sorensen (Atlanta Olympian), Canyon Ceman (AVP beach player), Matt Lyles (USA international) and Brett Winslow (USA international). On the bench was Loy Ball, the eventual starting setter for the U.S.A in Atlanta and possessor of the infamous 'anger is a gift' tattoo..

The strange names did not stop at Canyon Ceman though. The Great Britain team favourite was our mate 'Coley Cyman'. He was a frenetic and very intense middle blocker. I was lined up against him in the USA match. He did everything one hundred percent while muttering constantly like a man possessed. He looked like he was on loan from Westpoint military academy with his marine haircut. You could imagine him at American training sessions with his coach stood over him in a tough drill saying.

"Do you want to quit?" Coley shouting back. "No! man, I got nowhere else to go."

He was now on the opposite side of the net to me and had made it his mission to give me a hard time. Everything he or I did came with a comment. He talked at me the whole time I was on court. If he beat me on a shot he would let me know, 'sucker' etc. If I jumped with him and the ball went elsewhere he would go berserk at me. Using his favourite line 'you're ass was mine on that one junior'.

I had to wait until set three to finally roof him, he went even more crazy. He came and stood staring me out face to face and said. "I'm gonna own your ass now boy!" My arse wasn't for sale, but to be fair I would have traded him my 'ass' for one of his playing shirts. I kept my composure however and the only thing I could think of saying as he stared into my face was an old John Cleese line, from a Fawlty Towers episode called 'Waldorf Salad'. "It's all bottoms with you Americans isn't it." I said, doing my best Cleese impression.

It was wasted on him, he called me a 'faggot' and went back to hitting the ball very hard and generally acting like a loony. The match progressed in a similar vein to the others and Tommy Sorensen was amazing. He was the cannon and launched himself repeatedly from the back row canning the ball on the floor. I was powerless to stop him at the net, in the end I was substituted and Chris Hykiel came on and made a historic block on Tommy. One he won't forget. It was always like that for the whole team. Like a bad game of golf, you end up living for the one good shot in your hundred or so swings to make it a top round again and go home happy. Chris went home happy and he still talks about it, boring bastard! You wouldn't catch me doing that.

At the end of the game we tried to swap shirts. They were not having any of it and we were gutted. We had lost three nil, but we had realised a dream and played against the States. All irrelevant in the greater scheme because we walked away from the game empty handed, setless and shirtless.

A week on from the USA game and after the men's volleyball final, Chris Hykiel walked into the dining area looking pretty pleased with himself. Slowly, while stood teasingly in front of the team table, he removed his tracksuit top like an ugly six foot eight table dancer. Underneath was the prize we all wanted. He had an American shirt on. Damn it! Chris had traded with the yanks and got himself a whole genuine 1988 Olympic style playing kit. I was absolutely devastated. I asked truculently where he had got it from. It transpired that he had gone into the sanctum of the U.S.A volleyball apartment and they had agreed to trade while they all packed to fly out to the Pan American games the following day. According to Chris though, that was the only window of opportunity and they were refusing to trade anymore stuff.

I just couldn't accept that. I knew the Games was going to be my only taste of competition at this level as a player. I wasn't about to let the chance go and look back on it with regret. I headed back to my room and got some kit, then marched off to the U.S.A apartment. When I got to the rooms they were all still packing. I went into one room, in it were Tommy Sorensen, Matt Lyles, Canyon Cemen and the team captain Nick Becker. I was suddenly very conscious that I was stood, uninvited in their room. Tommy Sorensen was sat on a chair with a towel round his shoulders. Nick Becker was shaving Tommy's head with clippers, giving him a marines mohawk. They all looked up.

Tentatively I asked if they had anything to trade, you could have cut the atmosphere with a knife. They were obviously fed up with visitors just wanting to get hold off U.S.A playing shirts. They all continued to stare at me, until Canyon Ceman said "Sorry man, we're all traded out."

That was it then, short of attempting to mug four massive blokes, my one and only chance of obtaining the 'Mona Lisa' of volleyball shirts had gone. I was clinging on though and surprised myself by beginning to speak. I do not know where it came from or why I chose to say it, but I am glad I did. "Er, I didn't come for shirts." I explained and they looked up puzzled. Shit, I was on the spot, what had come for? I looked around for inspiration and it came to me in a flash.

"I want to swap this Great Britain shirt for that pile of Tommy's hair." I said pointing to the fresh cuttings on the floor.

There was a short pause and then they all started to laugh. Matt Lyles, now a medical doctor in the States, stood up.

"That was cool." he said still laughing. "Let's go see what I got in my kit bag."

I followed him to his room, passing Coley Cyman packing his bags, complete with mad commentary.

He gave me his training kit, shirt and shorts. It wasn't the actual playing kit, but it was pretty close. They asked me if I wanted to go for beer with them, I went off and fetched some of the other lads and we headed off to the bar with Canyon Ceman, Nick Becker and Matt Lyles. We sat and chatted about volleyball and we bored them stupid, asking about Steve Timmons and Karch Kiraly. Top evening, for us anyway.

To this day Chris Hykiel and I have an ongoing shirt battle. I will send him spoof letters from window cleaners appealing for cheap rags for their business. They write that they have heard about Chris's collection of tatty old volleyball shirts and did he want to sell them for a quid?

Chris will reply in a similar vein. It is he though that can win every argument. He simply produces his bone fide U.S.A playing shirt, still in pristine condition, and with that I lose. One day I am going to steal it and burn it, but don't tell Chris.

The USA game over, we headed into a play-off pool as one of the worst teams, but not the bottom pool. We had been placed in an original playing pool with one less team, so we could only go into the play-off pool for ninth to thirteenth.

Team morale in the next week through to the close of the games plummeted. The on court players became a little separated from the bench players, even some players who were playing got disillusioned. Three players Michael Boxwell, Mark Arme and Nigel Gallaway hadn't been on court at all. Team meetings with the coaching staff were getting tense, players openly showing there annoyance at not playing. All of us had been away from home for two weeks already, one more to go. That added to the strain.

The final week was interesting. We got out to see more sports, including a fascinating quarter final waterpolo game between Russia and Canada. The game was violent. Waterpolo is one of those sports that people tend to assume is non-contact and bound by fair play ethics. We watched the game sat next to the British waterpolo squad players, they explained the rudiments of the game and the nature of the contest. The waterpolo hats stop ears being removed and head injuries, players wear two pairs of trunks and a 'box', the umpire can't see what goes on under the water! The game we watched didn't disappoint, the Russians and Canadians went at it. It was a blood-bath. Several expulsions, some blood and competitors fighting with each other at the end of the match. The Russians won the game, but did themselves no favours. The Canadians, well they highlighted the volatile nature of sports people at the top level. They left the game and went back to their flat in the Games village. They called into a D.I.Y shop on the way and purchased some sledge hammers, goodness knows how they got them past security. Probably threw them over a perimeter fence and collected them from the inside. On arrival at their flats, one above the other, they had a huge party and began to smash their way through the flooring and walls between each flat. By the next morning they had destroyed a fair amount of their accommodation and planned to complete the job after their last game.

When the team left to play that game the next evening, the organisers went into the flat to check out complaints of noise from the previous evening. They found the mess, which had also made the building structurally unsound, builders were called in to shore up the walls. The Canadians, were escorted from the changing rooms after the game by Police. They were taken to pack and then frog marched on to a bus which took them straight to the airport and a flight home.

We played Belgium next and got up for the game remembering how close we were to them in training. The game was really unpleasant. They had a couple of arrogant thugs playing for them and edged the first two sets. Set three and our team mood boiled over. We decided to go after the two Belgium prima donnas, shouting at them, pulling faces and laughing. They responded in an unexpected way and became aggressive and abusive, but with twice the ferocity of our attempts. We lost the last set 15-13 and as we shook hands one of the Belgians grabbed my hand hard and said. "In Belgium I am a football hooligan, outside I will kill you."

I told Neil what the player had said and the other players and we headed off to change, sure enough they were waiting for us. A small scuffle occurred and was broken up by the coaches. We were ordered to stay in our changing rooms until the Belgians were escorted away from the sport centre.

It was a privilege to play the next game against the South Koreans, they were wonderful to watch and really tough to compete with. We generally played poorly in sets one and two. Set three came and the coaches decided to bring on Mark Arme. Mark is an aggressive, but quietly determined player. He was brought on to court to play through four and two weeks of frustration at not playing were unleashed on the Koreans. We lost set three 15-12 and Mark was almost unstoppable, he jumped so high and hit the ball so hard, siding out time and again. He was a one man team. After the game the South Korea team and coaching staff all came to him and shook hands and bowed to show their respect for his game. Mike Rhodes presented Mark with the South Korean pendent to commemorate his play.

Our last game, was a difficult one to prepare for. Four or five players had had enough and were looking to leave after the last game. Our original plan to head down to Whitfield and take the tournament, was falling apart. Indonesia sounded like a game we could win, but morale was low and no player was really up for it.

Sure enough we went down 3-0 again and didn't seem to care. We swapped shirts with the Indonesian's, who were a tremendously skilled and fast outfit. That was it then, it was all over.

We had a few days before the closing ceremony. In that time three players went home early, the squad atmosphere was negatively affected by their departure.

My mood didn't improve when I got trapped with Mike Rhodes and Craig Torrance in a lift in the village. We were at the far end of one of the tower blocks and heading off to the bar. The lift just jammed between floors. Mike told us that he was a claustrophobic, we laughed. But, he wasn't lying. He was so bad in fact that he was part of a study in Scotland into people who didn't like confined spaces. Craig Torrance, still not convinced that Mike wasn't joking said, "I was stuck in a lift for hours once and seeing as we're up the other end of the building we probably won't get found until morning."

That was it Mike flipped. He was white and sweating, actually he was no longer Mike. He began to bounce around the lift walls getting more and more agitated. After a short bout of shouting and banging on the doors he collapsed and laid in the corner shaking. That was a little unnerving to say the least. Finally, after forty five minutes of pressing the emergency buzzer, we got an answer from the caretakers office. They came and crow barred the doors open and within seconds Mike was back to normal.

The closing ceremony, although spectacular, was a stark contrast to the excited expectations of the opening ceremony. Those of us that attended enjoyed it and the concert in village afterwards, where 'The Beat', remember them? 'Mirror in the Bathroom' and all that, played a brilliant set.

The next day, me, Neil, Mike Rhodes, Craig Torrance and Nigel Gallaway set off to play Whitfield 1991. The only squad members able to make the tournament we went through to the final and attempted to extend the Games experience further. Deep down we all knew it was over. I headed back to Chichester on the train, the Sunday evening after the Whitfield final. It was a long ride.

For weeks after the event I couldn't really get myself going. All I wanted to do was talk about the event. If I had ever got the chance to do it again I would have known how to make more of the experience, but in my heart of hearts I knew that kind of competition was out of my league and it wouldn't be happening.

It was a good run through. Three years in the squad, twenty nine international games, some good friends and a great time.

Look at that leap. Fergus No.8

Nick and Carole Smith

WSIHE 1986

Top row: Nick Robinson, Andy Hinds (Monty), Me, Andy Hebert,
Paul Andrews and Nick Smith (coach)
Bottom row: Ashley Brown, Tony Robins, Fergus Leslie,
Andy Wild and John Waters.

WSIHE 1987
Top row: Nick, Paul, Me, Jim Barker, Andy, Rob Harley, Simon Coleman
Bottom row: Si Northcott, John Waters, Fergus, Ashley Brown,
Paul Phelps

WSIHE GOLD 1988
Top row: Rob, Matt Lawrence, George Zorzi, Me, Jim,
Chris Harty, Simon
Bottom row: Fergus, Steve Richards, Paul, Si, Mark Harris.

Fergus setting, tongue out.

Me serving, tongue in.

Phil Newton
Liverpool legend

WSIHE Women 1988

The un-rivalled thrill of the World Student Games opening ceremony, Don Valley Stadium, 1991.

Helen Sharp accidentally sets light to a local hill, the track, herself, some officials and finally, the Games flame.

Craig Torrance and Chris Leshniak (Post student days)

Keith Nicholls

Bobby Stokes

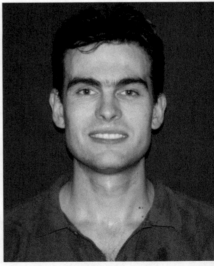

Chris Hykiel (Polonia die hard, tall bloke and international shirt theif)

© B.M.Totterdell

The first British hit of the 1991 Games. Neil gives me acres of court to find and I manage to bounce it off the German blockers head.

My Games pass. It gave me food, a bed and two weeks of really big blokes hitting balls at my angelic young face.

British students in the Whitfield final 1991 versus Malory. Neil setting me, Nigel Gallaway (No.7) looking on and Richard Dobell, Alex Bialokoz and Donald Deans not bothering to block me. Cheeky buggers!

The main man. Mikey Rhodes surveys the carnage after one day in our Games village flat. The mess is 10% mine and Neil's and 90% Mikes soiled underwear.

Still standing: Me, Roger Hunter, Mark Arme, Hyks, John Lyall, Andy Marshall, Steve Milne. Floored by Mikey: Mike Boxwell, Neil Withington, Alex Gunn and Mike out of shot.

Matt Lyles training shirt and playing shorts, kindly traded.

Neville McKenzie (Lucifer)

John Scringeour (Sweem)

Auds and Mo posing for Volleyball News, at Tenby.

Lisa Arce (left) and Christine Schaeffer (right), under pressure from Mo and Auds in Chile.

The wonderful La Serena beach, Chile. Stadium viewed from my room at the hotel complex.

My hotel view of Copacabbana beach, Rio. nb: I did actually leave my hotel rooms while at the events.

A right pair of silly sods. The Canadians Becky Rose (left) and Monica Lueg.

Me signing another sponsorship deal.

Gary Duncan livin' la vida loca.

Sean Pool

Stuart Watson. An educational player to watch, you always seem to learn some new words.

One of the best photos I've ever taken. Richard Dobell (front) 'the pec monster' and Alex Bialokoz 'Dr Block', Tenby 1994.

Tim Hollis and Grant Pursey (passing) at Weymouth. The best team I've played against on a British beach.

Vince Joyce (VJ) many people's 'King of the Beach'.

Rob Kittlety (Nib) great value on the sand.

My other favourite photo. It took me hours to talk Jurek Jankowski into this pose and a solemn promise that I would never publish the photo.

Steve Draper, you know the old saying. "If he's smiling he's just about to shout at a ref, if he isn't smiling, he's already shouting at one."

Me and Neil taking time-out between severe beatings at Weymouth 1990 to pose for some beach god publicity shots.

Julian Banasiewicz making a great dig in the Tynemouth final 1993. Just before asking if our opponents were internationals.

Ever wondered where Clayton Lucas got his jump from? I had to stick a ball down my shorts to make Clayton's over developed arse muscles look normal in this photo!

© N. Lamont

Top southpaw, Chris Eaton,
letting me block him at
Bournemouth 1998.

One of the guys I really
enjoyed watching play,
Andy Cranstone.

© B.M. Totterdell

Ian Fairclough (Billy) former No.1 British beach player and beach president.

Crowd favourite, Greg Gwinnet and Rose Clarke on the stand

The good looking half of the world famous 'Beach Allstars' band, Chris Brook (left) and Steve Allgood. Rock 'n' Roll..............

Phil Davies (Bear) and Danny Wol

Anthony Roberts (left) and Andy (Mushy) Jones.

Me swinging on one of Clayton's nectar sets, Weymouth 1999.

Going after the impossible. Clayton goes all out to make the play.
Weymouth 1999.

© B.M.Totterdell

Tristan Boyd bombs another jumper, Weymouth 2000.

The 'keeping' still comes in useful, Weymouth 1999.

© B.M.Totterdell

Big hits for show, but passing for dough, Weymouth final 2000. Digging my way to the MVP Award.

Time-out. Laying it on the line to the Polonia lads, 1998.

Me setting for Wessex in the
2000 K.O Cup Final.

Phil Allen one of the best
volleyball men I have met
in my 15 years.

Wessex K.O Cup Final squad 2000
Top row: (left to right) Tim Hollis, Chris Whitbread, Gus Courtiour, Alex
Burt and Me.
Bottom row: (left to right) Mike Randall, Morph Bowes, Phil Allen and
Clayton Lucas.

113

Richard Dobell's favourite cartoon. I know it is because he told me just before he felled me with a friendly right cross.

© B.M.Totterdell

My favourite non-playing photo. Me interviewing Jeff Williams, Audrey Cooper and Vanessa Malone for Sky T.V.

114

Chapter 3
Mo and Auds

How I got there...................

1995 was to be the most demanding, challenging and all said and done rewarding seasons of my career. It signalled a move for me into a higher level of coaching and a taste of the many unseen hardships that come with that. Coaching Mo Glover and Audrey Cooper was an opportunity which presented itself at a good time in my career and an opportunity I learned a tremendous amount from. It's important to explain where I was in volleyball when Mo and Auds invited me to coach.

Since 1993 I had been coaching Team Solent in division 3 south of the NVL. In the 1993-94 season we went undefeated to the championship, as player coach I won the Reebok Player of the Year award for that division and pretty much all was well. I was also having a great time playing Sussex league with Hastings V.C, Dave Gander and the lads, a volleyball club founded by the Civil Service and fielding mostly Service players. It was a crazy time. Training with Solent Tuesday and Thursday, driving to Hastings (3 hours away) to play local league, then back to Solent for weekend national league.

I had moved into a role at Solent which suited me as a developing coach. I was one of the better players in the team, having played division 1 volleyball and they were desperate for a coach for that season. The consequence of this was a relatively trouble free season with the kind of success that smooths the way for change and progression.

We competed really well in division 2, but as with any coaching job the issue of player management, especially concerning court time began to surface. I had encountered player problems in all my other coaching jobs, but my experiences in 1995 were at a higher playing level than I had worked at before.

I really admire the coaches who deliver the goods. They deliver player performances, teams and ultimately results. So often the tortuous journey of player management, difficult decisions and programme development that go to producing the above go largely unreported. All coaches will be with me on this one when I say that every job will throw up a series of tough calls. If you have a problem with players not liking you, with feeling completely isolated at times and with frustrating behaviour from your players, you will not go on to make it as a coach.

In 1995 I may have felt like the proverbial dog's under carriage, but it was to become brutally apparent to me that I was light years away from making it.

My first real concept of a great coach was Doug Beale, the USA coach who brought Gold to the men's team in LA 1994. I have read many of his articles and for me his book 'Gold' is the definitive book on the job of coaching westernised players.

I say westernised players because the former communist and eastern block coaches were always working with the might of the State behind their every ranting outburst. Karpol the former USSR women's coach, now current Russian coach is the definitive case in point. Mentally abusive and sometimes physically abusive time-outs are common place to the point where the crowds at the games begin to howl their disapproval at his treatment of players. That kind of approach cannot succeed in the western forum of player choice and power.

All Beale had to work with when he took over the lowly World ranked USA men's team was his vision of potential Olympic glory. He had almost no funds, no players and little support, but in only four years he produced a Gold medal side. The Soviet boycott was technically not an issue as the USA had despatched them in the previous World Championships, heralding their arrival on the World stage.

What Beale achieved was nothing short of one of the most incredible coaching feats of all time. In reaching that goal of Olympic glory he had his fair share of hardship. He firstly cleared out the 'old guard' then went to the university squads to appeal to the youthful ambitions and drive of those players.

His first test for the squad was to take them on a outward bound team building experience in Colorado. This proved to be the first watershed in the process that eventually produced one of the best teams to ever grace the World volleyball stage Kiraly, Timmons, Powers, Dvorak, Berzins and Buck.

It was Beale's conviction that drove the team, himself and those around him on. The decisions he was faced with and the choices he made were in the final analysis, correct. However, even with hindsight, they feature as tremendously demanding.

Beale lost players because of his approach. He did not rant and rave, but simply imposed a set of standards on the team that he reached through negotiation with the players. He lost the players that did not fancy camping in the snowy peaks of Colorado. He then lost the players that could not agree to a full-time programme training in the morning, working part-time in jobs he had found them (bank clerks, check-out boys etc) then training in the evening. Sinjin Smith and Tim Hovland left at this point. Both had begun to sense a beach revolution and Smith was often offered lucrative modelling contracts which meant weeks away from training.

Now for all Smith's amazing achievements in beach volleyball it is Kiraly who has the three Gold medals. That must hurt.

Perhaps Beale's most incredible decision involved Steve Timmons, generally acknowledged as the most destructive hitter of his time.

Beale had changed the system of play, it was he who revolutionised volleyball in the 1980's with a shift to a two passer system. It was he that having had the vision of only two passers in the rotation made Kiraly and Berzins pass fifty consecutive 'good' balls at the end of every single session. This could sometimes result in training finishes at 2.00 am in the morning as passers and servers contested the fifty passes. It was Beale who told Timmons he was not good enough to fill a spot on the USA roster.

As a coach Beale must have known his players so well. Timmons was sent away with the university squad to the Pan American games. He could have lost one of the king pins of the 1984 triumph. Timmons though reacted exactly as Beale wanted. He trained harder and tried to develop all the elements to his game that the coach needed.

Kiraly remembers Timmons was away from the team for some three months travelling and playing elsewhere. In that time he managed to put on some twenty pounds in bulk and had acquired an extra few MPH to his hammer. The rest as they say is history.

Having admired so many great coaches Velasco of Italy and Alberda of Holland to name but a few, you try to emulate some of their qualities. My constant failing as a coach has been a lack of consistency and in 1995 at only 27 years old, a lack of real conviction in my coaching ideas. This results in my sometimes curt handling of certain types of peripheral player while conversely treating the more influential players with kid gloves, not wanting to offend or destroy the channels of communication.

With Solent I was their most successful coach. I had a group of players that were equipped to play division one, supported by a set of peripheral players who worked hard for their places. With that came my first serious coaching challenge.

A well known player in the Hampshire area, was concerned about his lack of court time. What made it worse was he usually sat on the bench while 'I' played in 'his' passer swing hitter position. For the most part if you leave players to moan and bitch, without challenging them about their behaviour or views, they will come good for you when you need them. You have to watch your back though.

Joop Alberda, the Dutch coach, has a series of simple statements that he applies to the players in his squad. One of them is trust. He trusts the players to prepare themselves and behave appropriately. You have to do that as a coach, much as you want to you cannot control everything and everybody.

This style of coaching means that every so often you will be forced to take on divisive players. You may have to talk to them and find out what the problem is so you can begin to deal with it. You may have to challenge a player on their behaviour, so much easier said than done. All of this is vital to the coaching process, but by it's nature time consuming and mentally demanding. Most players argue like they want you to back down, to agree with them. When you do they instantly lose respect for you because you are not a strong coach.

My sole approach to these problems at the time was completely autocratic and sometimes still is. My view was, if you want to be part of the team, this is how it is. If you do not like that then you can get lost.

When the Solent player phoned me at home for about the third time in a week to complain about his lack of court time I had exhausted my limited range of counselling skills. In what has proved to be the first of many player encounters I had found my Achilles heal writ large. I can talk with players, I can listen to players, but as soon as they are dishonest I lose it.

His third phone call, clearly about his lack of play in the starting six, had now become a thinly disguised attempt to tell me that the team was not behind me and there was apparently considerable support from the team for him to play instead of me. I tried to process the information rationally and no matter how I thought it through it still came down to one factor. The player was furious at not playing, fair enough, I can live with that. He was expressing his anger however, through a dishonest statement about the team.

When a player fails to grasp the basic concepts or see the facts as they really are I do not think any coach should have to deal with that in a reasonable manner. That is when players, and their families incidentally, begin to cause trouble.

The Solent bloke was a good player, a solid passer hitter. Unfortunately, he was over weight, not particularly fit and only experienced at a relatively low level. He was demanding a place on court, over me. I was a good five inches taller than him, I could jump way higher than him, hit harder and was one of the best passers in the country at the time (Now I'm being dishonest), I was also the coach, and he wanted to start ahead of me. My resulting 'piss off!' followed by putting the phone down was not my best move.

When I did it again five minutes later after he rang back, it didn't improve the situation.

He took his gripe to the team, following the next game, a game he was suspended from. The team also told him to 'piss off!' and after a rather edgy committee hearing when I was invited to explain why I had sworn at a club member, my case was upheld and he was removed from the club. However, the realisation that this coaching lark was a whole Pandora's box overflowing with more and more problems the higher you went, began to dawn on me.

My time with Solent continued with relatively few hiccups after that. The team was a real eclectic mix of players, but it seemed to work well. All the players were reasonably well established and had varying levels of experience. Dave Brewer (former Fire Service international), Rob Smith or Boff as some of you may know him (former Wessex and England squad player), Steve Draper (former Wessex player and my beach partner at the time), Dr Bill Brocklesby (former Oxford varsity player and laser physicist at Southampton University), Dr Tim Bugg (former Cambridge varsity player and Professor of Enzyme Chemistry at Southampton University), Tony Fazakerly (a big hairy bugger and former Havant Pumas player) and local boy Graham Sault (now with Wessex in Division 1), who with more access to decent coaching at an early age could have made it at international level.

It was a pretty good team overall, but like any squad we needed a setter to function. The team was held together by the team character, who also doubled as the setter. Dave Martin was a rotund little man from Australia and was a very successful optician in his own right. Because he was from Australia the lads, with stunning originality, had nicknamed him 'Oz'. Oz was a top bloke, didn't give a shit about anything and despite his lack of fitness and height could set as well as most division one setters I have played with.

I remember training one evening, I was passing and Oz was setting. He was chuckling away at the net and kept looking at me as I prepared to pass. I set up to pass another ball and Oz shouted at the serve to wait a minute. He ran over to me and said, "Who is just about to serve?"

I had been struggling to really focus on objects as far away as the other end of a volleyball court, for some months. I squinted furiously, unbeknown to me. But, I knew my team well and was getting pretty good at silhouette identification. I guessed right, but reluctantly had to admit that I really couldn't see all that well. Oz advised me to pop in to see him for a sight test.

When I called in to see Oz he was very thorough and explained that I did in fact need glasses to drive and watch the television. He was right, everything improved when I got the specs.

With regard to the playing difficulties it was not and still does not affect me a great deal. Oz however, offered to give me a pair of light prescription contact lenses to experiment with. He handed them over at the end of the Tuesday training session along with explicit instructions on how to put them in.

The next training session evening arrived. I have never been bothered by eyes and was happy to have a go at putting in the lenses, I assumed that it would be a piece of cake. One hour later, still poking myself repeatedly in the eyes stood in front of the bathroom mirror and swearing my head off, I suddenly had complete and utter respect for any person who has ever worn contact lenses. Every time I tried to put them in they slipped out, this problem was accompanied by a hideous stinging sensation that felt as if I was trying to slip a salt and vinegar crisp into my eye.

Finally with snot dripping from my nose and both eyes streaming I got the bloody things in and was ready to head off to training.

The improvement was amazing. I really felt I could focus on players and the ball, the usually dark dreary gym seemed to be full of colour that night. The team trained and I had a good session, I could only put it down to my new amazing lenses. The session finished and I thanked Oz for my new self-contained eyewear, but admitted that it had taken me an age to get the damn things in and I was worried about retrieving them from my eyes. He offered to firstly help me yank the lenses out, then go through the rudiments of putting them in again.

Oz searched around my eyes, for what seemed like an age. What the hell had happened? Had my new lenses burrowed their way into the surface of my eye, was I about to be rushed to hospital for surgery. Oz began to giggle. "Sorry mate, but there's no bloody lenses in there." He smiled.

I headed home confused. One hour of eye poking, blinking furiously and stinging pains, but I was still deficient in the contact lens department to the tune of two. They must have fallen out during the session. On arrival at my house I went up to the bathroom to clean my teeth. On the floor by the sink was a small patch of water, I bent down to take a closer look, in the water was one contact lens. In the sink, next to the plug-hole, was the other. They never left the house.

In January 1995 I travelled up to West London Institute, now under Brunel University, to interview Mo Glover and Audrey Cooper. The interview was going to be the lead feature in my newly launched magazine, Volleyball News.

The magazine was an attempt to fill the gap left by Volleyball World, the former E.V.A publication. It was a good idea in principal, but with relatively little experience in the field I was going to find out the tough reality of trying to get such a bold project off the ground with such limited resources. In the meantime though I was an editor. I set about the task with gusto and began to line up interviews and features left right and centre.

The reasons for picking Mo and Audrey as the first issue main story were simple. I had long admired what they were trying to do in qualifying for the 1996 Olympic beach volleyball event and as characters they stood out a mile on the domestic tour.

The girls kindly gave permission to appear in the magazine and so it was that I found myself heading into the West London gym, notepad and camera close to hand.

The interview itself went well and both players talked very openly and frankly about their playing experiences to date and their dreams for Olympic glory. The information was fascinating. Here were two women, both in full-time employment, slogging it around the World to compile enough points to qualify for two World Championships and then an Olympics.

To achieve their ranking of thirteen at that time they had held down their respective jobs, somehow convincing employers and sponsors to share in their vision and hot footing it to countries like Brazil, U.S.A, Chile, China and Japan.

You just have to admire that kind of commitment, the Atlanta reward was well earned and completely deserved.

The last point raised by the Mo and Audrey in the interview, was the need for a coach to look after the team. The need for a coach was becoming more and more apparent. Most teams in the top twenty had coaches and Mo and Audrey saw appointing a coach as the next logical step to help them maintain their hard earned World ranking in what was increasingly becoming a pre-Olympic bun fight for places.

I stated that I was interested in the coaching position. It was a coaching position that I had looked at closely. The girls had little joy trying to convince other coaches to work with them and actually travel to events with them. I must have been the only coach to confirm an interest in doing both those things.

Part of Audrey's ability in volleyball is her mental toughness. This mental toughness comes through in many ways, sometimes a quiet determination, sometimes an aggressive streak that is rarely witnessed in women's volleyball. On this occasion it was a polite, but completely noncommittal acknowledgement of my interest.

The girls asked me to an interview at Audrey's house to discuss my coaching credentials and my plans for the team. Their only real knowledge of me was as a generally psychotic young player who moonlighted as a stand-up comic come magazine editor. To be honest as the realisation of the scale of what I had applied to do, coach a World Series and potential Olympic team, dawned on me I was struggling to see how they were going to take my offer seriously.

Imagine the impression if the England team turned up at the next World Series tournament technical meeting and the tournament organiser asks if there are anymore questions. The English coach stands up and says "I say, I say, I say, did anyone here the one about referee, the promoter and a tub of industrial strength sun cream?" Cue foreign teams looking bemused.

In glorious twenty twenty hindsight I was too young. My lack of real beach coaching experience was going to be a factor, but on the plus side I did have coaching experience in general and a real interest and desire to work at the highest level in the sport. I did have a sports degree and good all-round knowledge of volleyball and my own clipboard.

It was the positives that I presented to the girls, while carefully acknowledging the areas of my coaching that would require development. I had no idea how a World Series event ran, what the protocol was, what the media demand was and importantly what the role of the coach could actually be while at a tournament.

This has to go down as a real high point in my volleyball career. Mo and Audrey liked the information I presented and I was appointed as their coach. I drove back to my house with thoughts of World Series beach volleyball and although two years off, the Olympics, swimming around in my head.

The job was going to throw up many challenges over the coming months and serve as the most incredible learning experience of my coaching career and probably my life.

The main difficulty for me, while actually at the events, was the fact that beach volleyball, rather like tennis does not recognise the status of the coach. The coach only has limited access to the tournament site and more often than not would have to rely on their ability to network to get into those hard to reach places. Something I was going to have to learn and learn fast.

Sky's the limit.................

It began. Just like that, one day I was player coach with a division two national league side, the next I was a national team coach. The demand began immediately and took a couple of weeks to get used to.

I was contacted by Marzenna Bogdanowicz, the team manager, to discuss my sponsorship clothing requirements and pass on some invaluable information about the events I was going to be involved with. Her final gem however, was to let me know that in two days time I was due on Sky Sports live Saturday afternoon television show with the team. Sky were building a sand court in the studio and while the girls demonstrated the game I was going to be interviewed by Suzanne Dando. What a crazy week.

We turned up at Sky Sports, in South London nervous about the programme. We were due to be on all afternoon and although the show was going out against Grandstand which guaranteed small viewing figures, it was still live and if I accidentally said 'bollocks!' or 'shit!' to Suzanne Dando, I would just die.

Anyone that knows me will know I get nerves. Before matches, tournaments I get anxious. Yet somehow the thought of live television with all the trappings and potential traps was not worrying me a great deal. We arrived at Sky and met the shows director, still no problems, in fact I was looking forward to it. Normally I cannot eat before a big game, I feel too nauseous, but as we were led to the canteen I was feeling good and helped my self to a tray full of food. It was free and I was going to fill my boots.

We took our seats at a table, myself, Mo and Audrey. I loaded my fork full of food and just as I put it to my mouth I was aware of some people stood right next to me. The director said, "Hi guys, this is Suzanne, she will be presenting the show this afternoon."

Suzanne, put her hand on my shoulder. My shoulder. "Look at all that food, I never used to be able to eat before I went on air." she laughed looking at my tray.

My earlier bravado evaporated and nausea and nerves set in. Miss Dando joined us and I sat there like a starstruck teenager, staring at my tray full of food which now had all the appeal of a tray full of saw dust.

We got made up and went into the tiny studio. The beach court was in there, next to the main set up where Paul the presenter sat and was having his hair fixed yet again by a patient assistant.

The court was a tiny area of sand, a net, some deck chairs and just in case anyone thought beach volleyball was a serious sport a bar complete with tables and brollies.

Once we had seen the studio it was off to the green room to wait for our call. In the green room we met Mark Lawrenson waiting to do discuss the soccer results, Kate Howie the M.P and Sean Udahl (Hampshire spin bowler) waiting to talk cricket. We politely answered all the usual questions. Does the ball hurt when it hits your arms ? Do you really play in your pants ? and so on.

Finally, our call came. We had been watching the show on a monitor in the green room and it was difficult to equate that with the small garage lock-up studio we were just about to walk into.

I was dressed in a Speedo shirt and rather too bright shorts and reviewing the video recently I was sporting a really big hair do. I looked like a new romantics lead singer on the front cover of smash hits just about to play a game of squash.

The girls were in bikinis, I guess we were going all out for the kill. That has always been the problem with beach volleyball in the media. The sex always seems to get in the way, but at the same time is a valuable selling tool.

I and other players have been approached to do various dodgy things to do with beach volleyball over the years. I have even been approached by the Sun to pose for some topless mixed volleyball shots. I didn't agree to because I have my principles and the E.V.A said they would ban me if I did. Some players were also approached at Ruislip lido a few years ago to appear in a 'lunchbox volleyball' programme for a cable show in London. In a Radio Five Live interview in 1998 the presenter summed it up when she started her interview with, "Right! let's go for the lowest common denominator..." and then proceeded to ask about the sports now legendary sex appeal.

The interviews on Sky Sports went extremely well. Suzanne Dando was very professional and myself and Mo and Audrey managed to answer the questions without getting tongue tied or saying 'bollocks!' or 'shit!'.

We finished the show off with a pretend game on the mini court, under strict instructions not to get sand anywhere near the £20,000 a throw cameras. The game was Mo and Audrey versus myself and Miss Dando. It is a great little piece of television and I am talked into showing the recording to my lecture groups every so often....yeh! right like it takes much talking.

Chile, lovely, and only thirty eight hours door to door, tell yer Mum..........

The tournament in Chile was to be my first coaching test and it was looming, like a huge coaching present just waiting to be unwrapped.
We had a couple of weeks to prepare as a team. The girls had not been near sand for some weeks and in the middle of winter we had no chance of recreating a lush golden, warm, Chilean beach paradise for training. A chilly beach was going to be about all we could arrange.

As the cameras were switched off and rolled away we said our goodbyes and reality hit home. We were stood in what looked like a jazzed up garage in south west London, with a patch of sand on the floor. All of a sudden Chile, the skinny bit on the arse end of the Americas, seemed like it was on the other side of the World. When I got home that evening I had a look in my atlas and bugger me! It was on the other side of the World.

The team trained as well as it could, in sports halls and weight rooms. Then one day, following the Sky broadcast, Sutton Coldfield Rugby Club rang to offer their indoor 'sandbox' training facility as a potential winter training venue.

The girls and I jumped into the car, the weekend before Chile, and steamed off to the midlands. The gesture by the club was a kind one. It would have been a useful one as well, but for two things. Firstly, the brick building was so cold that it could have been passed by the environmental health inspectors as a meat locker for an abattoir. But, what the hey! Cold is cold, so we started to warm-up.

The second problem became obvious almost immediately. There was definitely sand involved in the 'sandbox', but it's consistency and colour was similar to that of a Sumo wrestling ring.

The centre director walked in and we thanked him politely for his offer of the venue. Casually I asked what the 'sand' was, he very proudly told us that it was oiled kiln sand (the stuff they cast metals in), mixed with horse-hair of all things.

I could almost see the fear etched into the faces of our World Series opponents. Players who had mistakenly flown down to Chile a week early to acclimatise to the heat and practice on the La Serena beach sand. While the British team had trained on the real thing. 'Hey! Karch, you ever trained on oiled kiln sand mixed with horsehair?....no?..........poof!' That interesting experience under our belts it was time to pack for Chile.

This trip was going to be a big test for me on a personal level. The coaching of course held many challenges for me, but the first real problem was the fact that I absolutely detest and fear flying. My hatred comes from a single experience of flight as a fifteen year old boy, returning from a trip to stay with a French penfriend in Corsica. The plane having hit an air pocket plunged downward, I was terrified by this. This terror was compounded, however, by a large American woman seated next to me on the plane and now hanging on to my arm and screaming "Oh my God! we're all gonna die!" The plane juddered and began to climb again and the American resumed her demolition of her airline meal. While I was scarred for life.

Now I was driving up to Audrey's house to meet the girls and then head off to Heathrow in a taxi. On my journey to Audrey's, around the M25, I sped under the climing and descending planes at Heathrow and tried to rationalise that I would soon be back on a plane.

In acknowledgement of my phobia Mo and Auds had masterminded the biggest cover-up since the make-up artist on Joan Collins last photo shoot ... ooh! get me.

I headed to the airport with the firls version of our impending travel plans firmly in my head. It was going to be a breeze, seventeen hours straight flying, then hop off at Chile. No problem.

So it came to pass that we were stood at the check-in. The girls sorting bags and tickets and me standing like a big pink idiot feeling pretty good. Eurphoria had set in following my popping a flight tablet and throwing a double scotch down my neck. I was ready to board.

Mind you, we nearly didn't get that far. I had arrived at Audrey's house in the sort of hyped up state that a vertigo sufferer would have got into prior to a skydive. I walked through the door and into a silent house, something wasn't right. Audrey was sat down with an ice pack on her knee, looking distraught. It was the very same knee that had given out on her earlier in the day and had not improved. I was required to make my first real coaching decision. A decision I was forced to face while battling with an unbelievably selfish feeling of absolute relief at the fact I might not have to fly. The ball was in my court and now I didn't have to fly if I didn't want to.

Luckily some sort of rational perspective returned and I swung from the feeling of a condemned man reprieved, to despair for Auds and the realisation that my coaching debut on the world stage would probably be curtailed.

I spoke carefully with Audrey. After all, shouting 'brilliant! I don't have to fly now' would have definitely been a poor coaching move. I found myself suggesting that we should still travel with the intention of playing and if the knee didn't recover after a seventeen hour rest we would withdraw, but take the opportunity to scout the other teams for future reference. We were already in the main draw after all, that was worth $1500. I heard my words floating in the air and suppressed an urge to tell myself to shut up!

We agreed the plan was sound and now we were stood at customs checking on to the flight and I was looped. So looped that I still didn't register the initial destination of our first flight. It was only on the plane that my initial substance induced euphoria began to fade and was replaced with a quizzical, nervous feeling.

I began to look around the plane and certain things didn't seem to add up. The plane was small, not what I had expected from a transatlantic vessel. There was also something wrong with the leg room, there wasn't any.

How the hell was I going to suffer these cramped conditions for seventeen hours. I was uncomfortable already and we still hadn't left the ground. With panic setting in I turned to Mo. She looked at me and smiled her usual everythings all right in the world smile. "You alright then?" she chirped.

"Yeh? I suppose so, but this plane seems really small for a transatlantic flight." I moaned.

The game was up. It was time for Mo and Auds to spill the beans, finest South American beans as it happened.

Travelling, as you all know is an extremely expensive process. Flying around the world to compete on the FIVB Beach Volleyball World Series is really expensive. 12 events, 24 flights, 48 nights hotel accommodation. You do the maths.

Marzenna's job, therefore, was to arrange discounted air travel, a job she was very good at and with the aid of the B.O.A she got some great deals. The flight to Chile was an absolute steal. This type of travel, however, rarely comes with a British Airways logo stamped on the side of the plane.

So I found myself, with my team, aboard a Spanish plane. I like my planes to look modern, with bright up to date colour schemes and interiors, it gives me an added reassurance. Unfortunately, this companies planes were mostly old and squeaky. The decor on this craft was beige and dark brown and reminded me of the layout of the Crucible Theatre during a World championship snooker final in the 1970s. Which was highly appropriate because that was when this particular plane had been built.

I tensed up in my seat. I really needed another drink. That was the answer, another drink served to me by some dusky mediteranean beauty of a hostess, who would then mop my fevered brow. While assuring me that Captain Sanchez had flown many thousands of carefree miles during his long distinguished career.

I looked up to attract one of the hostesses attention, scanning around the plane as I did so. The sight was not pleasant. Unfortunately the airline seemed to exclusively hire their cabin crew from a small Spanish village. A village who's population had inherited and passed on a dog ugly gene which had been mixed with their pig ugly genetic pool. I waved to a wizened old spinster with a face like a smacked bum. She headed towards me, with small sparks leaping of her polyester cabin crew uniform. Uniforms that looked as if they had been purchased as a job lot from the Crossroads prop department after the series was canned.

She shuffled towards me and eventually arrived at my chair. It was difficult to tell whether she was going to take my order or spit on me. I asked for a glass of red wine to help with my nerves and she smirked at me, seemingly delighted at my uncomfortable situation. She then said "No!" And wandered away to prepare for take off.

The fact I was sat on an aeroplane being waited on by, as Kathy Norman (the Australian beach player) would say, the cast from the bar in Star Wars, was bad enough. The full horror of the special flight deal, however, was just about to be explained to me.

Mo has an uncanny knack of laughing uncontrollably while grabbing your arm when she is about to tell you something you probably don't want to hear. She was not wrong, I definitely didn't want to hear this.

The reason we were on such a small plane was that it was a short haul flight to Madrid. Madrid for Christs sake, not only were we flying to the other side of the world, but we were starting off by going in the wrong bloody direction.

"So let me get this straight." I said to Mo slowly. "We fly to Madrid, then we jump on the 'big bird' and head for Chile."

She laughed even harder. I knew I was in trouble.

The deal was to fly to Madrid (2 hours), pick up a jumbo to Rio (13 hours), change again and fly down to Santiago over the Andes, ring any bells? (8 hours) and finally get onto a small jet and speed off to La Serena beach and the event (2 hours). Bummer!

I was now a wreck. There was only so much drinking I could do and it was becoming obvious I was going to have to face the majority of the journey in 'real time'. The concept was terrifying.

Thirteen hours into the Rio flight though, I was starting to get used to this flying lark. The cabin crew were still miserable sods and the in flight entertainment, popular on so many modern airlines, had passed vessel by. They favoured the pull down screen onto which was projected a series of terrible films all dubbed into Spanish. The only thing of value was a small display on the cabin wall which depicted our planes progress over South America.

Just as I began to relax it emerged that the Spanish pilot still had a wee trick up his sleeve. He seemed not to feel any communication was ever necessary with his passengers. No polite information about speeds, times, flying heights and the ground temperature of your destination. Mind you, if you have just left Spain which was 'scorchio' and you were now approaching Rio which was 'very scorchio' what's the point?

Approaching Rio, however, a short "Ladies and gentlemen we are now going to plummet three thousand feet over some mountains into Rio airport!" Would have been appreciated. As we shot down at a rate of knots, I went white and broke into a cold sweat, Mo was sat in the chair next to me and started laughing again.

We changed at Rio and got back on what looked suspiciously like the same plane, with the same cabin crew, although identification between the hostesses I suspect could only really be achieved by the use of dental records. There were almost no passengers on the flight down to Santiago. It was spooky. Some Chileans and us, sat on a massive jumbo jet. We spread out and fell asleep across chairs, before I knew it we were on our approach to Santiago airport. Santiago was evidently also, 'scorchio'.

Having come through customs at Santiago airport we set about finding our next flight, a jet to La Serena beach. As we moved through the vast marble concourse, with all our luggage on a trolley, I noticed a stange sensation like a buzzing in my legs. Accompanying the buzzing was the sight of locals, taxi drivers, baggage handlers, check-in clerks and concession stand operatives, beginning to lay down on the floor. After twenty hours of flying your ability to process information was impaired. Figuring out why several hundred people should start to lay day in an airport was beyond my comprehension.

Then, within seconds, the trolley began to snake back and forth. Even with the heavy bags on it I was finding it difficult to control, let alone keep pushing. The suspended marble concourse that we were on began to sway and the decorative airport lighting started to shake visibly and it wasn't the litre or so of Spanish red wine I had consumed mid-flight. We had stepped off the aeroplane and into an earthquake. Luckily before any real panic set in it was over, as quickly as it had begun. The locals stood up again, completely non-plussed by the events of the last few minutes, and went about their business.

Having recovered some composure we arrived at the check-in for our next flight. The woman on the desk smiled and told us we had another four hour wait for the flight and then pointed out of the main airport terminal and about a mile down the road to a small wooden shed. She told us that was where our next flight to La Serena Beach departed from.

"Thank you" we said, I don't know about the other two, but I didn't actually mean it.

We went into Santiago on a bus. It was a good chance to look around and pick up the Chilean vibe. We only saw a small part of the city, but what we saw was fantastic. I suppose Santiago was like many major cities, large imposing stone buildings, thousands of people going about their daily lives. It varied from London, Paris and Hamburg, other cities I had experienced in that it really had what I would classify as that South American feel about it. Many locals were in traditional dress, but not for tourist purposes. Small stands selling fruit and vegetables were dotted around the streets. Austere policemen with side arms or machine guns strolled amongst the crowds. Young people shot around on mopeds with no crash helmets. Groups of people were chatting and so many seemed to be smiling and laughing. There was undoubtedly a friendly atmosphere to the city environment.

It was a wonderful hot sunny day, the sunlight bounced off the faces of the large stone buildings, emphasising light and shade. Most buildings had coloured flags flying from the windows. In between the layout of the buildings were small square areas of grass, covered with people sitting, eating, drinking, talking and reading.

Having taken an hour to walk around it was time to eat again. I had my Spanish phrase book and was determined to get us sorted out for food. It wasn't until we wanted to eat that we realised we had not seen a single restaurant. I went to ask a taxi driver where the nearest eating establishment was. He seemed to understand my question and pointed us into a large featureless building across the street.

We went into the building and I repeated my question to the commissioner in the foyer of the building. He pointed upstairs and said 'siet', seventh floor.

Our mood was still good, we had nearly arrived at our final destination, Santiago was beautiful and amazingly Audrey's knee, although not in brilliant shape was not hurting as much and she managed the stairs relatively easily.

We arrived on the seventh floor and walked straight into what can only be described as some kind of huge Civil Service style canteen. This was clearly not a place where we could get food. So we set off back to the streets.

Eventually we found a restaurant and ordered pizza's, ate them, then set off to the small shed-come-airport annexe we had been shown earlier in the day.

We checked in and waited to get on the plane. I looked around to get my bearings and for the first time, since taking the coaching job, felt like I was part of something. A feeling that I suspect Audrey and Mo got when they first started competing on the World Series. Standing around the small departure lounge were a number of World Series players, mostly from the USA, that I recognised from videos, coaching books and the American magazine 'Volleyball'.

I was stood just feet from Elaine Roque and Gail Castro, No.2 on the WPVA tour in the States. Just across from them were two younger players Lisa Arce and Christine Schaeffer who were stood with one of the World's best known women's players, the now legendary Holly McPeak. The only player I could not see was my all-time beach heroine Karolyn Kirby, who was rumoured to be playing, but with a new try-out partner in the shape of

Deborah Richardson after her regular partner Liz Masakayan blew her anterior cruciate ligament in a tournament, only weeks earlier.

The players were called to board. To my relief the plane was a really nice, if small, modern jet. I took my seat on board and found that the seat next to me was spare. At the last minute another player boarded and a pair of legs appeared next to my chair. The player who owned the legs eased herself into the chair and unsmiling made herself comfortable.

It couldn't be happening, not to me. Yet again my luck was in, of all the planes and all the spare seats in all the World, Karolyn Kirby had just sat down on this one, next to me. Overcome with excitement and completely star struck I couldn't resist an introduction. "Hi!" I said, smiling at Ms Kirby. "I'm Simon Golding, the British coach."

"Hi!" she replied. "I'm Karolyn Kirby and I'm going to sleep."

With that she put her personal stereo on and slept the whole journey. A journey incidentally which goes down as one of my strangest flights. We took off and stayed almost vertical, climbing steeply we were told to get over the mountains, more bloody mountains. The hostesses, not Spanish airlines, therefore nice people, struggled up and down the aisle and threw orange juice and peanuts at us. After half and hour we lurched forward and descended steeply towards La Serena airport. The hostesses didn't have to collect any empty trays, they all slid forwards and into a pile just behind the cockpit.

We finally touched down at La Serena. We left Heathrow at 7.00pm the previous day and 24 hours flying later we had arrived.

La Serena was a tiny airport that looked like a retirement bungalow in Bournemouth, surrounded by a picturesque range of mountains, which looked almost holy with the setting sun casting a soft pinky orange light across the peaks, offset by a beep blue sky behind them. It was truly stunning.

The FIVB minibus arrived and we all jumped on, me and ten female beach volleyball players, if the boys could see me now.

On arrival at the hotel we checked in and found that as was the case on most trips, the coach was not acknowledged and I could have a room for one night in return for most of my spending money. I was tired and nervous at being in a new place, so I took the room and would just have to rough it for the next four nights after that.

The hotel was fantastic, real luxury, with a great pool and facilities and a superb view across the road to the beach stadium.

First job was to get the players mobile so they would be ready for training the next day. In addition to that, to cover ourselves, I called out the local Doctor and reported to the organisers that Audrey had injured her knee get-

131

ting off one of the planes we had flown on.

We went down to the pool and Mo and Audrey exercised in the pool to work off some stiffness from the long journey. We ate after the swim and then headed up to Mo and Audrey's room to await the doctor.

He arrived and was instantly re-assuring. He explained, in perfect English, that he could find no ligament damage and felt that some anti-inflammatory treatment another nights rest and the use of a knee support would probably mean Audrey could play.

I jogged over the road to the stadium and booked out some court time for practice the next day. All three of us slept well that night.

The next day, after breakfast, the girls relaxed and I got a taxi into town to fulfil the other part of being the coach. I went to the pharmacy that the Doctor had advised me to visit, the chemist turned out to be his brother and he was expecting me. I was asked to wait while my prescription was prepared and a seat with a cup of coffee was brought out. I was then surrounded, could I spare half an hour to let them practice their English on me. Yes I could.

So I spent a very pleasant time sipping delicious coffee and listening to various people from the chemist to his cleaner, excitedly speaking English phrases at me. I corrected their mistakes and replied to their various questions and statements and they clapped delightedly, it was charming.

Before I left they demanded that I teach them a phrase in English. I taught them 'come on Leeds United'. My new students and various people in the store joined in and shouted at the top of their voices.... "Come on Leeds United!"

I left the Pharmacy armed with tablets, cream and a knee support. They did the trick and to our great relief Audrey was ready to train by that afternoon.

Training time is available to everyone on the main court, therefore it becomes like gold dust. When a court is booked to train at a tournament you will instantly acquire some bargaining rights, players and coaches who had previously ignored you, now wanted to talk to you and be friendly, hoping that they could 'share' your session.

It was vital to get the right mix of drills and scrimmage, after all Mo and Auds could have weeks between matches against top class opposition due to their returning home after each event.

The first team we came in contact with, were some of Mo and Auds old friends, the Canadians Becci Rose and Monica Lueg. We had court time and a male coach to hit jump serves at them. They had a huge bag full of brand new Mikasa beach volleyballs, it was deal made in heaven.

Becci Rose was an absolute loony. Loud, unfazed by the tour protocol and never willing to accept the affectations of the top players. She had seen a French and Saunders television show while on a trip to England. The show where Dawn French thinks she's seen Madonna on a film set and then proceeds to shout 'Madonna!' to see if the star would turn around. Becci used to do that at breakfast to the top seeds and then roll around with laughter if they looked up.

Her partner Monica Lueg was a former indoor international, to be fair it seemed like they were sometimes just on the tour for a laugh, although they did get good results now and again.

Rose and Lueg's claim to fame was their historic two woman block on centre court at the Chile event. Both players stranded at the net, Becci and Monica looked at each other and decided to jump. They were playing Karolyn Kirby and Deb Richardson which made it even more special. On seeing two blockers in the air Kirby couldn't think of a call, so Richardson just hammered it and Monica roofed her. Cue two Canadians screaming and running around the court in celebration, the crowd loved it and Richardson laughed, while Kirby, ever the professional, didn't.

With a days training under our belt it was now a chance for me to scout the potential first round opposition currently battling their way through the qualifier.

I felt that Christine Schaeffer and Lisa Arce would prove to be the most likely opposition and took some extra time charting their favourite side-out shots and block/defence combinations. Both players were big hitters, but not particularly mobile and if the block could be negotiated there was a good chance of getting the ball down.

Arce and Schaeffer were indeed confirmed as the first round opponents. Not really a good draw, the fourth ranked team on the U.S tour in the first game.

Up to this point Mo and Audrey had been cheerful and chatty and at twenty six years old I was naive enough to think this was business as usual. Things were about to change.

We got up on the morning of the first match, the girls were due to play second game, on at about 10.00am. Mo and Audrey had their game faces on. This meant a complete and initially unnerving change to absolute concentration. It took me back. Every good coach and teacher knows that the first part of successful relationship is to 'know your learners'. This was a vital part of the learning process for me.

We ate in silence and then moved upstairs to the girls hotel room to review the match plan. Most athletes have a way of behaving under pressure, some get silly and noisy, some get nasty and some go very quiet.

Audrey was incredibly intense and sat across the room from me on a big sofa. She looked so mean that I wasn't even sure that I should be speaking. I tentatively began to go through the game plan, the girls listened, but with no acknowledgement. I plugged away for the duration of my talk, in complete silence. When I had finished they both stopped staring at me, stood up and left the room.

I sat for a moment absolutely stunned at what had just happened. Neither player had shouted at me or walked off in the talk, so I just rationalised that it had gone well. This is where my inexperience was a problem and although I undoubtedly did some good for the team, there was so much more that I should have done.

I headed for the stadium, the girls were now on their own and to be honest I was relieved. I sat up in the grandstand that surrounded the centre court on three sides. It was an inspiring sight, looking down onto the court which resembled a Roman coliseum where gladiators were doing battle.

My mind wandered back to events earlier that day. It had really phased me to see two players so intensely focused on the job in hand. To be honest I was shit scared of facing them again after the game, especially if they lost and my game plan was responsible.

I needn't have worried, the girls played an unbelievable game of volleyball. The match plan was sound, but the execution was superb and I sat and watched Mo and Audrey cruise to a 14-9 lead. A huge upset was on the cards.

Then the age old phenomena of failing to take the last point raised it's ugly mug. The Americans, chiefly inspired by Arce's devastating jump serve, woke up and started to claw the game back. Mo and Audrey hung on, but there was an inevitability about the American comeback. Two English girls, relatively inexperienced in being matchpoints up on World class opposition, against two American girls trained to win in the blazing professional intensity of the indoor university leagues. The USA players were used to winning games week in week out to pay the bills. The Americans eventually, in one hour ten minutes, took the match.

Because the main draw was double elimination, lose twice and you're out, Mo and Audrey had another chance. They were gutted at the loss, having been in such a strong position, but they seemed to trust me now that my first game plan had held up. Against the Americans my game plan was neither here nor there, it was all down to the girls hard work, but four thousand miles away from home teams need all the help they can get.

In the next game in the losers bracket Mo and Auds were drawn to meet a Chilean local side. Although there was the pressure of travelling for thirty hours to lose and go out in the first morning of the tournament, the girls were used to dealing with this. The local team were in it for a laugh and the girls got through 15-1, with the local crowd booing them with a friendly edge. The main advantage of this was guaranteed support from the Chilean spectators in the next match.

The girls, having made the second day, returned to the hotel. I stayed on to watch the last matches to scout information for the following day. I was building up an excellent file of team statistics for game plans.

My money had run out so I checked out of my room and paid the bill. I gathered my bags up and headed off towards Mo and Audrey's room, there was a sofa I could sleep on.

I arrived at what I thought was the right floor and the right room. The door was ajar and I could hear noises. I burst in through the door laden with bags and stood transfixed. I recognised one of the Italian team, a tall blonde girl with a face like a Spanish air hostess she was naked and straddling the national team coach. He was also naked. To complete the scene the other player in pair was sat on the sofa over the other side of the room, casually reading a book, she could have been knitting such was her nonchalance at what was occurring just yards from her.

The fornicating couple slowed down, they didn't stop, and turned to face me. I was frozen to the spot.

"Hi!" said the blonde girl, smiling at me.

"Hello" I replied, eager to comply with etiquette.

After what seemed like an age of staring at the frankly grotesque scene I managed to stutter.

"Wrong room, sorry!"

"That's OK! no problem." said the blonde girl. The coach never even flinched and continued his work and the girl on the sofa just kept reading. I turned and sprinted from the room, I could hear gales of laughter as I ran down the corridor. I was never able to look them in the eye at breakfast again.

The next day arrived and it was the same intense scenes as day one, I didn't find it any easier to deal with.

The girls breezed past a poor Mexican team to set up an afternoon clash with Japan 2.

I had done my homework on Japan 2 and without doubt the game against them stands out as one of my most pleasing coaching experiences to date. The type of experience that makes you believe you should be doing the job you have chosen to do. It makes you feel justify in your belief that you are up to coaching at that level. As usual in sport, this feeling is all to often short lived, delivering a smack in the mouth at the next opportunity and forcing to question all of the things you just thought you had found the answers to.

I had scouted Japan 2 thoroughly and had picked up a clear pattern of side-out shots. The right side player tended to favour a short chip shot over the blocker or a deep cross, where as the left side player went short cross or deep line. I instructed Audrey to stay mid court to run down any shots their opponents attempted outside of the normal routine shots and got Mo to fake block at the net, then back off into the two zones I had highlighted on my scorepad and hopefully collect the softer shots. There was no hopefully about it. I sat in the stands and watched with absolute pride as Mo and Audrey executed to perfection.

We returned to the courts and took some inspiration from the presence a group of ex-pats in the main hospitality area of the Grandstand. They identified themselves with a small union jack tea towel draped over the railing and lots of encouraging shouts.

The Japanese girls went to their favoured shots and there was Mo seemingly just stood there waiting for the ball. They changed to their second shots and Audrey hoovered the ball up with ease. Mo and Auds raced into a 9-0 lead and never let go, winning the game 15-3 and guaranteeing 9th place in the tournament, a third days play and $4,000 U.S in the bank.

We headed back to the hotel, very happy indeed, especially because we were drawn to play Arce and Schaeffer again for a place in the top 7 the following morning.

It wasn't until we were sat eating our meal that evening, lasagne as I recall (more of that in a minute, quiet literally), that Audrey's brow suddenly furrowed.

"Bloody hell!" she exclaimed. "We're supposed to be flying home tomorrow afternoon."

We had all completely forgotten the return journey, what with all the success of the previous two days.

We debated the situation. If the girls won, we would miss the flight and be stranded on the other side of the World. The decision was easy, try to win the game and sort out the mess after that. We finished eating and went up to get an early night.

I awoke the next morning with a stabbing pain in my stomach, remember the lasagne? I certainly did. I felt nauseous and thought my guts were going to explode. Audrey had exactly the same symptoms, but Mo didn't and she hadn't had the lasagne. I sat and waited patiently as the girls got ready. Mo felt too nervous and Audrey too ill to attempt breakfast, as the game was at 9.00am the plan was to get ready, review the game plan and head for the stadium.

I sat with my stomach cramping badly the victim of a terrible dilemma. The girls still had to finish off in the bathroom, cleaning teeth, putting hair up in scrunchies. I just couldn't get into the loo, if I did I would have rendered it out of bounds for some considerable time. I couldn't do that to my team. My toilet efforts tend to have a half life at the best of times, but I was convinced that with my upset stomach this delivery would not be classified as human.

The other difficulty was the location of the hotel toilets in reception, they were only a five minutes walk, but I surmised that would be about four minutes forty five seconds too far. I would have filled my shorts before I got out of the room.

So I stayed on the sofa, just praying for Mo and Audrey to go and leave the coast clear for me. Audrey must have been suffering similar problems and she had a match to face, it didn't bear thinking about. I had once played a soccer match at primary school when I had a bad stomach. I jumped to head a ball and with a great exploding fart I crapped myself mid-air, much to the amusement of the other players. I have a vivid and painful memory of being carried off the pitch by the referee, in tears. Me not the ref, although his eyes were probably watering. Suspended in my shorts was a lolling mass of diarrhoea. Not a pleasant experience and one I have tried to rule out of my life since. I wouldn't have wished it on Audrey in a World Series game, centre court.

They finally left the room. I was so relieved I was nearly crying. I stood up slowly and gingerly made my way to the bathroom clenching my buttocks like I was in the front row of a Kenny Gee concert.

Ensconced in the sanctuary of the bathroom and seated on the loo it happened, like a volcanic eruption, I clung on for dear life just waiting to ride out the storm. It seemed to go on for ages. Then the smell hit me, you know it's bad when you can't stand it yourself. That's the beauty of farts. You can let one go in a car full of team mates, common practice believe me, safe in the knowledge that despite the other passengers retching you will remain unaffected.

On this occasion I just sat holding my breath as the last tremors subsided. Then with impeccable timing there was a knock on the bathroom door. It was Mo.

"Simon, I've left my sunglasses in the bathroom, can I come in and get them?" She called through the locked door.

"Er....No....errr.....hang on! I'll find them and bring them down." I whimpered. I was panicking now, this couldn't be happening. I had spoken so I had to take another breath.....OH MY GOD! and I was breathing through my mouth.

Mo was insistent, she wanted in. With no thread of dignity left and the threat of another severe attack of Versuvius bum I elected to remain where I was but make semi-naked dash to open the door. If Mo wanted her glasses, which probably had no coating left on them by now, she could have them.

Mo walked through the door and was instantly felled by the stench. I just sat, resigned to the hideous situation and watched helpless as Mo, also nearly helpless, waded in and began to search frantically through her bags. She was now holding her breath and having already got a lung full was determined not to repeat the experience, but her air was running out.

Working as a macabre team I sighted the specs and pointed them out. I have never seen someone look so grateful. Mo grabbed them and legged it slamming the door behind her and then taking a huge audible breath. She remained silent about the whole incident and we never mentioned it again, until now.

It was not the ideal start to an important match day and both Mo and Audrey were a little out of sorts. Consequently the Americans took the game 15-9, leaving the girls in a creditable ninth place and as we subsequently remembered enabling us to get to our flight home.

The journey home, with no event at the end, was just one long slog. It took thirty eight hours door to door. We left La Serena at 5.00pm, on arrival at Santiago airport we discovered that our flight to Rio had been delayed through to the following morning. We were stranded in Santiago airport for the next twelve hours. I got a hotel phone number from the FIVB representative back in La Serena and then spent a comical half an hour on the phone to the local recommended hotel. I was unable to get any sense from the hotel receptionist and obviously fed up with me she passed the phone to someone else. An English speaker came on the line and in a broad Canadian accent asked who I was. I explained our predicament to the person now on the end of the line which, as it happened, belonged to Mark Heese the Atlanta Olympic beach volleyball bronze medalist no less. He tried without success to get us a room, when he was unable to secure any accommodation for us we chatted about 'beach' for a while and then under my instruction he passed on a couple of choice phrases to the hotel manager. That was it then, we were sleeping in the airport terminal.

We spent an ugly night trying to sleep, but keeping a shift of watches over our bags and ourselves. Finally 7.00am came and we boarded the flight to Rio. Rio to Madrid overnight and the short haul flight with all the early morning commuters, Madrid to Heathrow.

138

Blame it on Rio..............

Having returned to England we had only a few weeks to prepare for the World Championships in Brazil. I couldn't quiet believe I was going to be in Rio, not only at the World Championships on Copacabbana beach, but in the famous beach stadium that I first saw at 2.00am on Transworld Sport ten years earlier.

Again we flew Spanish and again not straight there. Heathrow to Madrid, Madrid to Washington, then Washington to Rio.

We were picked from the airport by an FIVB car and headed down to Copacabbana beach. The drive was amazing, a mixture of main roads soaring above the city on flyovers and smaller winding town roads through a series of urban outposts.

Finally we hit the main highway to the beaches. We were rewarded with an amazing sight and one I will never forget, towering in the distance, but still completely dominating the landscape was the statue of Jesus on top of the mountain. We were definitely in Rio.

To get to the beaches, still out of sight from the highway, the driver had to take us through the infamous Reboucas (pronounced Heboucas) tunnel cut into the mountain range that surrounds the coast. The taxi driver solemnly wound up the car windows and communicated, via some dodgey sign language, that we should not put any part of us outside the car. Evidently, as we discovered later from the Australian players, bandits were not averse to chopping off any limb with jewellery on it as cars sped by.

Having arrived at Margate, Weymouth, Bridlington, Sandown, Bournemouth, Poole, Barry Island and Tenby I was of course prepared for any beach in the World. However, the imposing sight of the Rio coastline took my breath away. The sand stretched away from for miles along, then towards the sea for hundreds of yards, soft white clean sand. It reflected the intense sun and lit the whole scene.

Where the sand finished the main pedestrian walkway started, for the entire length of the beach the street is paved with black and white chequered paving slabs, creating a stunning effect. The walkway was as wide as the M1 motorway and covered with market stalls, joggers, roller-bladers and tourists. There were people all over the sand and many in the seas surfing fluffy white breakers.

Exactly as I imagined, on the first section of the beach every fifty metres was a beach volleyball net. Some were being used for volleyball and some for the football version of the game, the sight was fantastic.

From the edge of the walkway, stretching across four lanes, was the coastal highway which you had to cross to reach the hundreds of beach front hotels. We eased around a curve in the highway and there it was, the Copacabbana beach stadium, my personal Wembley. It was a huge structure and literally right on the sand. Flags of every country competing adorned the upper reaches of the seating area and a causeway suspended fully ten metres over the highway, connected the stadium to a regal looking hotel.

The taxi continued on past the stadium and drew up at our not inconsiderable hotel. We checked in and then went to explore.

The guide books for Rio had described a completely different South American experience to that of the friendly, relaxed and open culture of Chile. The Police, armed as in Chile, were supported by troops. They hung around in ominous looking groups on street corners. Smoking and surveying the passers by. Set back from the main highway and hotels were the smaller side streets that the guide books warned us about. A favourite trick of some of the local criminal element was to get a small kid to run out and start kicking you in leg, any tourist that gave chase down one of the small dark alleys would then be mugged. While we were there we heard several gunshots. A local man was shot dead in a skirmish with Police in a small alley just one hundred metres from our hotel.

On a walk back from the stadium on my own on day three I was assaulted by a small boy, he came running up to me shouting and absolutely wacked me as hard as he could in the shin, then stood challenging me to follow him and take revenge. It really hurt and I made a grab for him. He was not quick enough and amazingly I caught his arm, he struggled and belted me again. I let him go and he ran off.

Over the other side of the highway, next to acres of sand, there was no sinister underworld just a 'life's a beach culture'. We tended to walk to the stadium on that side of the road.

We attended the technical meeting that evening. The FIVB took us along the coastal highway through Ipanema beach and up into the exclusive And expensive cliff top regions. They entertained us with a wonderful buffet at Rio's most exclusive ocean side hotel and briefed the players on the forthcoming World Championships.

On the bus we sat next to the Czech Republic team. Hudkova and Tobiashova were the only Czech players on the women's tour, they were a little aloof so any small talk was difficult. The older player, who talked least, tended to attend any evening function, including evening meals in the hotel in various flowing evening dresses. The players would all be dining in tracksuits and shorts, so dressing up for dinner always looked so out of place. Making her appearance even more bizarre however, was the fact that the garments she wore were always brightly coloured and flowing. She used to look like Princess Margaret attending a 70's function. On the bus she glided up the gangway in her most hideous choice of dress to date. It was layers of chiffon, trailing down like a bunch of handkerchiefs that someone had been sick on. She behaved like a princess and regally took her seat. It was a show stopping statement and explained the whole strange charade at each meal time. While those players around her paid her polite compliments on her wonderful cutting edge fashion talents I had to look out of the bus window, fighting off a massive attack of the giggles. She never spoke again.

All the regular players were there, but it was the Brazilian's who really stood out. Quieter away from home, they took over the show as hosts in their own town. Jacki Silva and Sandra Pires, Olympic Gold medalists, graciously moved around the hotel checking that players were OK! and were being properly taken care of.

Sandra Pires, is an amazing beach athlete, but also a real character off court. She seemed to know everybody as she moved around chatting. Over the coming days you would see her on many occasions dancing around the hotel, the stadium and the courts listening to her personal stereo. She also had one unnerving habit. A fan of various punk and heavy metal music she would often come charging over to us with her earphones blaring and demand a translation of the English lyrics in the song she was listening to. I tended to just make stuff up, not being overly keen on trying to explain the meaning of 'pink torpedo', 'flesh tuxedo' or 'bum cakes'. (Spinal Tap fans forgive my paraphrasing.)

I booked training time at the courts adjacent to the stadium for the next morning. We walked down at 11.00am to train, it didn't feel oppressively hot mainly because it was a dry heat. Next to the courts was a large digital clock which displayed the time, date and finally temperature. The temperature read forty three degrees, it should have felt warmer.

The practice court was pristine with water in coolers, shaded areas to cool down and a bucket of new balls to train with. We waited for the Brazilian's to finish their session, watching in awe at their ball control and power hitting. They finished, we exchanged a few pleasantries and then took over the court.

Only then did the temperature become hideously relevant. The one thing that the practice courts did not possess was a water cannon to wet the sand and cool it down. We stepped out on to the court from the shaded area and within five or so steps the sand was literally burning our feet. I jumped around like a cat on a hot tin roof, well like a cat in a large burning hot litter tray anyway. It was excruciating, we ran back in the shade to the cool sand. That short burst of exercise had induced copious sweating. It was now apparent that the two days to acclimatise, all we could afford, was going to be nowhere near enough.

Mo and Auds donned small neoprene sand socks and I put on my very own white sports socks. I really looked like an Englishman abroad. It was still uncomfortably hot and by the end of our half hour session, all we could manage in the heat, I was conducting the session while stood on a towel.

We slept well that afternoon and then headed out for food with the German team and some Australian players. The hotel had recommended a small restaurant just around the corner. It was a lovely little place, very friendly and relaxed. We ordered food and tucked in. All in all it was a pleasant evening. I returned to my room and drifted off to sleep.

At around three the next morning I was woken by sirens in the street. I looked out of my window and down to the brightly lit highway twelve floors below. There was an ambulance at reception and three figures hunched in blankets were being loaded into the vehicle. By lunchtime the next day I found out that it was the German coach and two players who had eaten with us the night before. They were rushed to hospital with food poisoning and given some injections to calm things down.

I didn't really get back to sleep and by 5.00am with day light saving in operation, it was already light outside. I opened the curtains in my room, expecting to see a sleepy seaside town beginning to come to life. Sod that! Rio was wide awake and had been so for some time. The beach was crowded already and every court was full of volleyballers and soccer players.

I got my shorts and a vest on and sauntered down to the courts. It was fantastic, lots of noise, players shouting and throwing themselves into pre-work games, quite literally. I walked slowly along the beach enjoying the variety of sporting action. The standard of the volleyball was good, not outstanding, but solid. It was the soccer volleyball that amazed me. Played on a Volleyball court, the players mounted the ball on a little pile of sand behind baseline and then kicked it over the net for service. The two players on the other side then had three touches to return the ball. I expected to see all out chasing around as players sliced volleys or misjudged headers, but it was nothing of the sort. With incredible skill and accuracy the players mostly executed three perfect touches using feet, thighs or heads to make the shots. The ball after travelling fifteen meters from the other side of the net would be volleyed usually using the feet for the first touch. The other player would move in to play the ball close to the net and more often than not would head the ball up for their partner. The partner would then run in to attack the ball, sometimes with a header and sometimes with a really spectacular bicycle kick comfortable in the knowledge that they had deep white Copacabbana sand to land on. The skill level was truly stunning.

I stayed and watched one particular match which had attracted a big crowd. There were hundreds of people sat around the edges of the court, really enjoying the game. It was still only 6.30am. I looked at the players and thought I recognised the shortest man on court, he looked very familiar. He was stocky with straw coloured hair and looked to be the most skilful of the four contestants. Then it came to me, it was Zico the Brazilian soccer star. Now retired, but clearly still in great shape. I turned to the boy sitting next to me.

"Zico?" I enquired, while pointing in the general direction of the court.

"Si!" he nodded looking at me indignantly. Bloody tourists! Why did they have to check with locals to identify soccer gods.

It was frustrating, I had no pen or paper to get his autograph and the hotel was too far away, so I contented myself by watching him play. I am no stranger to meeting my soccer heroes. My step Granddad Doug Hawes, a wonderful man and sadly no longer with us, was a former employee of the Football Association. Every year we would attend the Amateur F.A Vase where I got to meet the likes of Bobby Charlton, Tom Finney and Billy Wright. They all had a real presence, there was something about those soccer legends that made them stand out from the crowd. Zico was no different.

The World Championships were due to start and we had a good first round draw. Remember, I said that sport poses new questions just as you thought you had all the answers ? Well day one of the championships was going to give sport it's next chance to set me the most ridiculously hard exam paper it could think of.

Still high on the result in Chile we went into game one with confidence. It was a tie against the Mexicans that Mo and Auds had beaten convincingly in the last event. They won the game reasonably well again.

From my place in the coaching dug out, level with the sand and with thousands of chanting Brazilian's above me, it was a fantastic experience, I was in the Copacabanna stadium at the World Championships. Everything seemed so perfect. I took a long look around the stadium before I headed back to the main hotel to meet the players and discuss the next round game plan. It was just so amazing, ten thousand people in seating banked high into the deepest azure sky. Offset against the blue sky were the yellow, red or green T-shirts handed out by the sponsors. In each corner of the stadium was a Samba band, beating out rhythms and playing popular Brazilian folk songs. It was something to see it on television, but there was no describing the feeling of being there. I wished I could have called Fergus and told him, but we had lost touch in about 1993. The first chance I had to tell him about the whole experience was this year when I contacted him via e.mail at the school he now works at on the Gold Coast in Australia.

I walked over to the hotel, still not quiet believing that I was there and to be honest not fully concentrating on my next job, passing the game information to Mo and Audrey. I had thought long and hard about the next game, it was a really tough one against the No.2 American pairing of Castro and Roque. I had thought about the draw and had come to a straight forward coaching conclusion. The game would be at Midday, it was forty five degrees and the stadium completely protected the courts from any breeze. Mo and Audrey had to play two of the most confident and experienced players on the tour. My game plan was very simple, use the game as practice for service, but if you couldn't take straight points then don't worry about it and certainly don't push for a result that would be too difficult to achieve at this point in the season in such punishing conditions. Besides that, the losing bracket draw was good, with a game against the Indonesians and then probably the Dutch, both of whom the girls had beaten regularly.

My plan was about as popular as a fart in sauna. I might as well have slapped the girls in the face and told them they were shit and couldn't win anything. In my inexperience, I had presented what was very logical information in a very inappropriate way and the effect was dreadful. Both Audrey and Mo didn't like me a lot at that point in time. I had just asked them to throw a game, after all the training, the time and the effort they had invested in themselves, their coach didn't believe in them, just when they had another chance for a pop at the big girls. I was completely unprepared for their reaction and completely lost as to how to deal with the resulting reactions of the players. They both got up and with no acknowledgement of my being there the walked back to the stadium to warm-up.

They came out onto court ready to face the Americans and they played really hard. But, the belief that they could win had been taken away by my team talk. It meant they struggled to score points, but they sided out very well. Siding out was made easier because Castro and Roque were playing the energy conservation game. It could have ended in a win and made me look like the king of psychological coaching ploys, but it didn't. So, nearly an hour later the game was over 15-8 to the USA. Two very upset and annoyed British players trudged off the court to the hotel. Boy was I looking forward to the next meeting.

Eager to please I made my next crucial error and over analysed the whole Indonesian game plan for the next match. Indonesia had one big player and one small player, the big player couldn't set a jelly and the small player never hit hard enough to warrant a block. That was it, nice and simple. I managed however, to come up with a contrived game plan involving Mo blocking the big player.

I arrived in the hotel foyer ready for a rocket from the team, what greeted me though immediately told me that we were probably going out. Both players were in serious bother having been too long in the heat, working at too higher an intensity without enough water or acclimatisation time in Brazil. They looked in bad shape. I went through the game plan, a plan which would have put the team under pressure even if they were fit. They were barely able to listen, Mo was slouched in the sofa looking tired and Audrey was pale. It was bad news allround.

They went on court with the crowd supporting the Indonesians, it made the whole situation very difficult indeed. No matter how hard they tried they the girls couldn't execute the game plan. Late in the day they had the good sense to change their approach around and started to get back in to it, but it was too late, the damage had already been done and they were too exhausted to win.

We spent a pretty unpleasant two days in Rio before we flew home. All of us wanted to be back in England and away from the beach.

We landed in Madrid and once again I had a stomach upset, worse than Chile. By the time we got to Heathrow in the mid Sunday morning I was feeling ropey. I headed off down the motorway and after seventeen hours flying and with a bad stomach I stepped on court for Solent and had a blinder against Leeds, which we won 3-2. Following the game I was so ill I was taken to the tropical diseases unit at Southampton General Hospital where samples given and tests taken indicated some sort of food poisoning from one of the flights. I really hated Spanish Airways.

Clearwater, Florida.............

There was another five weeks before the next event in Clearwater, Florida. We trained well for the first two weeks. At weekends the girls would come to Southampton to stay at my house and train at Bournemouth, during the week I would head up to Ruislip Lido. By week three though something was wrong, as with every beach team you go through a rough patch before you come out the other side and start to function as a team. Mo and Auds were still a relatively new team and I guess I was just starting to find out that it my job as coach to help them sort out an hassles and focus on the job. An

145

unpleasant task for any coach and one that I didn't deal with effectively. It nearly cost the team everything.

They would get niggly with each other at sessions. Mo the more vociferous player would get angry and begin to shout, there were a few difficult moments at training. Audrey would go quiet and sometimes that was tougher to deal with. I should have been talking about it and finding out ways to help them play as a team, instead I chose to ignore it and try to carry on regardless. It was a dreadful approach and just when the team really needed a coach I was nowhere to be seen. So, for three weeks I would turn up at sessions, not sure whether Mo was going blow her top and storm off and scared shitless that Audrey was going to show up in a negative frame of mind and make communication nigh on impossible. The thing I never got to grips with was that this is what players do. All players have their way of behaving under pressure and most are happy to discuss it. I forgot this, forgot my own reactions as a player and just carried on, hoping it would go away.

Things got so sticky that I remember setting up the net for a training session at Bournemouth, with Mo at one end of the court warming-up and Auds at the other. Neither player speaking. I was in the middle trying to get the net put up, aware of the situation and completely at a loss as to how to deal with it. I was then suddenly and terrifyingly aware that in my rather troubled mental state I had put a peg for anchoring the net down in the sand and lost it. We had no spare pegs and consequently the net wouldn't have gone up, I felt sure that the players, who didn't look ready to tolerate a fool gladly, were going to kill me. Driving all the way from London to train with no net, because the coach had lost the bloody pegs.

I kept it to myself and tried to look like I was still working on the net, while frantically searching the sand for the missing peg. My hand hit something and after a bit of digging there was a peg, not our peg, just a peg. I was beside myself with gratitude at saving the session and myself a bollocking. I needn't have bothered. Ten minutes into the session and the pair of them were pretty pissed off with each other and me. Mo got so mad she just walked off and away along the beach. Audrey, was quiet rightly mad at me for letting it happen.

"Are you just going to let her do that ?" She shouted at me. I was, it seemed. "You're bloody spineless!" concluded Audrey. She wasn't wrong. It is funny to look back on now, but it wasn't a pleasant situation then, for any of us.

The journey to Clearwater was very tense. Nobody really that relaxed, but as any coach working with top level athletes will tell you it is far from uncommon. Good coaches can deal with it.

On arrival in Florida we had to find a car hire place and rent a automobile to drive down to Clearwater beach, approximately a five hour drive. We arrived at Orlando, after the regulation stop in Washington, at around 7.00pm. By 8.30pm we were in a car and on our way to Clearwater, still pretty much in silence.

We drove into Clearwater a typical American/Floridian seaside town. Hotels, restaurants, T-shirt shops and the beach. I had driven the whole way to enable the girls to sleep, we got to the hotel and as usual no coaches were allowed. I was handed a leaflet with the name of a hotel where I could get a room, the Spyglass Motel, evidently just two blocks away. Mo and Audrey headed up to their room and we agreed a 10.00am meet at the courts to train the next morning.

I headed off in to town to search for my digs, but when I found the Spyglass it was shut, with a note on the door saying ' phone this number to get John to come check you in'. I went to find a phone and got John, who was not happy at being phoned at 2.00am, to check me in. I went up to my room and got into bed, but I couldn't sleep, the journey the problems with the team and over-tiredness had all got to me. I switched on the television 2.30am and found sixty channels of rubbish. Then joy of joys I recognised a programme as I shot past it with the remote, I took the channels back and there on the screen was James Herriot with most of his arm up a cows arse, I suddenly felt very reassured and drifted off to sleep with 'All Creatures Great and Small' playing on the T.V in seedy seaside motel in Florida.

My sleep wasn't fitful, amidst dreams of plane crashes and arguments with players I was suddenly aware of being awake and stood up in my room, with a terrible unhealthy mechanical droning sound at my feet. I took a tentative step forward in the dark and stubbed my toe on something large and cold on the floor. I fumbled for the light and there in a mess of wires and dust, vibrating round on the tiles was the air-conditioning unit, which in my sleep walk I had removed from the wall and deposited on the floor, somehow without injury to my person. I turned the device off and pushed it back into the dirty cavity in the wall, it stayed there. I returned to bed, but it was 6.00am and I couldn't sleep, time then for an All-American breakfast.

I walked to the diner next to the beach stadium. It was a most excellent example of a typical U.S diner with every conceivable foodstuff of high cholesterol content imaginable and coffee on tap until you had the shakes. I was in heaven. I also noticed that for the first time on the trip I had relaxed, mainly because I was away from the girls. I ordered the works, talked with the old waitresses about the forthcoming tournament, parted with some ludicrously small amount of money and headed out into the early morning

Florida sun. I walked to the tournament site and looked around, I still had a couple of hours to kill before meeting the team.

I ended up sat in the FIVB event press box, courtesy of a wheeze I used to pull at accreditation.

"Hello, I'm the Editor of Volleyball News magazine, England. Did you get my fax?" The line if delivered with confidence and an air of 'I'm just off to interview Karch' was a winner. I always got my press pass.

Sat by centre court watching the players warm-up it was difficult to imagine how things could have been any better. With that thought still washing through my mind I turned to look at the man who had just sat down at my table.

"Hi!" said the man, smiling as he put an ice cold beer down in front of me. "I'm Sinjin, you the Speedo rep?" he enquired.

I knew it was Sinjin Smith, beach volleyball legend. I had hero worshipped the guy for the last ten years, but felt it would be rude to say 'duuh! I know who your are!' or slightly un-cool to leap up and run around the press box like an over-excited kid shouting 'it's Sinjin! it's Sinjin!

I opted for looking world tour wise, sat in my Speedo sponsored T-shirt, shorts and cap.

"Hi Sinjin. No I'm not the Speedo rep, I'm Simon Golding, the England women's coach." I replied.

"Oh OK!" he mumbled. With that he picked up my untouched ice cold beer and wandered off.

I met with the players at 10.00am and we trained with the Dutch, things improved a great deal. After watching a few other teams train we then went for a very pleasant meal in a restaurant full of players and talked volleyball for hours. A great finish to the day.

Day two of our stay was the first day of the main draw. Mo and Auds, still not fully recovered from the journey, were drawn against a Puerto Rican team. The Puerto Rican team consisted of two indoor National squad players, one of whom was the Captain. They came onto court confident, Mo and Audrey having been in good spirits the previous day had returned to their usual intense pre-game focus, but their whole demeanour suggested a team on the edge. I watched the first game with trepidation convinced that the first mistake by either British player would result in the resumption of the last three weeks hostilities. It never quiet boiled over in the Puerto Rican game, but the performance by Mo and Audrey's high standards was poor and the team went down badly.

This meant that they had to pick themselves up and keep winning to stay in. Unfortunately, as any beach player will tell you, some days you just don't want it badly enough. If you don't want to win and you are not playing well being on court is the worst place to be. Everyone has experienced this, you just get bad days every so often and there is almost nothing you can do about it. Mo and Audrey stepped on court against Mexico, a team they were seeded to beat, but all was far from well. Both players wanted to be somewhere else and playing anything, but beach volleyball. The game was over in minutes with both Mo and Audrey unable even to communicate on court, letting easy serves drop on the sand in front of them and making increasingly frustrating errors. The game finished a ridiculous 15-3 to Mexico. Mo dealt with it as she needed to and disappeared off to do her own thing, Audrey once she had calmed down stayed to talk with me. At that point though, I was powerless to do anything. The players must have felt terrible. For me it was the loneliest and most useless I have ever felt as a coach. I was three thousand miles away from home and doing a bloody awful job of looking after and coaching my team.

The last point of the Mexican game was a serve which landed midway between Mo and Audrey, neither player moved or called. They simply let the ball drop and walked off to shake hands with the refs and the opposition. In terms of defining moments, that was it for me. From that point on, having let my team disintegrate, I didn't want to do the job anymore. It was partly not having being experienced enough at the time to deal with the crap of the last month and partly because I genuinely felt that if I stayed I would not be able to help the team achieve their Olympic goal. I didn't think I could ever feel like that, but at that moment my missing out on an Olympic coaching spot just didn't matter.

Audrey and I spoke at length over the next day, but I think she knew I was struggling to stay with the programme. We got through the next few days playing crazy golf and watching the Clearwater event. The atmosphere improved dramatically once the pressure of results was removed. In all honesty though, it must have been the worst time ever for Mo and Audrey, their dream was under serious threat of failure and at that point I don't think either player could have given a straight answer on whether they were going to continue.

Various silly little things conspired against us during our stay in Clearwater. The worst was the long and expensive taxi ride Mo and I took to pick up our hire car. We took Audrey's credit card with us to pay for the car and of course they wouldn't except it without Audrey. Sheepishly we took another expensive cab back to the hotel and drew straws to tell Audrey what had happened. I lost, but to my relief she dealt with it very well and she and I headed off in the third expensive cab to finally secure the car.

We got back to Heathrow and I said my goodbyes. Two days later, after a tremendous amount of discussion with friends and family, I made my decision to quit. Even having watched Vince Joyce (the coach that replaced me and helped Mo and Audrey to the Games) proudly walking round the track at the Atlanta Olympic opening ceremony, it stillfelt like the right decision.

When the girls played and played so well at the Olympics for their ninth place, I felt proud that I was associated with a small part of that and I felt delighted for them. They sent me a postcard from Atlanta thanking me for my contribution, they didn't have to do that, it was a really kind gesture. Watching Sydney brought back some memories. Memories of the most amazing coaching experiences and the steepest learning curve I have ever had and the occasional thought of what I could have been part of.

Chapter 4
Beach Volleyball

First contact, February 1988............

With the exception of a few indoor volleyball die-hards, which I can number on the fingers of one hand, everyone I meet is fascinated by beach volleyball. Whether they be involved with volleyball or not, the Atlanta and Sydney Olympics, television advertising campaigns, Gabrielle Reece, seaside holidays and satellite television have shot the sport into the World's collective psyche. I am no different to the majority, I saw it and loved it instantly.

My first contact with the sport was through the television. It was 1988 and I was sat with Fergus on his living room sofa staring at the television and willing beach volleyball to appear on the screen.

Earlier that day, by a complete fluke, I had seen a television listing in a newspaper. I am sure we are all practised at the art of scan reading so you will not be surprised to hear that as I flicked my gaze over the T.V listings the word 'volleyball' leapt off a seemingly meaningless page full of words and smacked me right on the forehead. I slammed on my ocular brakes and reversed back across the page taking in the additional information 'beach', 'Transworld sport' and '2.00 am'.

So, at 1.50am we had turned on the television (we didn't want to miss a single point), switched to Channel 4 and sat, in complete silence, waiting for the minutes to pass. We had never seen or heard of beach volleyball before and our expectations for the spectacle were low. This probably made the impact even more memorable.

Transworld sport came on and our night vigil was rewarded as the announcer revealed that coverage from the World Beach Volleyball Championships in Rio would be the main feature on the programme.

If you're going to begin to play a sport, to become involved with it passionately and effectively, I believe you have to have to be lucky enough to see good role models. Coaching is important, teams, players and regional set ups are key. But all of them will be secondary to the influence of the role models we are fortunate enough to witness playing their sports. Role models that by human nature we will attempt to emulate. When I look back I suppose I have had my fair share of luck in this department.

In soccer as a goalkeeper, it began with Banks, but was dominated through the eighties by Clemence, Shilton, Ogrizovic, Corrigan and Jennings. Four out of those five, by the way, would not have allowed Maradonna to score, they would I am sure, have flattened the cheating little bastard as he jumped to handle home. You will all be able to immediately think back to your hero's and chart your developmental stages, alongside their efforts. That is what scares me about today's new sporting generation. What a choice of overpaid, abusive, posing smorgasbord is now on offer.

Little sport stars of the future could mould their games to that of a petulant millionaire footballer who's emaciated vacuous wife treats him like a fashion store dummy. If they are really lucky, they will be inspired to greatness by a sanctimonious group of greedy match fixing cricketers. With beach volleyball though I was yet again in luck and my first contact came through the box like an unbelievable vision.

The picture of the Copacabbana beach stadium, yes! a stadium built on the beach, took some time to decipher, such was the passion, the noise and the colour. As the parts of the vision fell into place though the effect was pure magic.

Fifteen thousand Brazilians giving it absolutely everything, dressed in complimentary 'Banco de Brazil' brilliantly coloured T-shirts, the fans danced, sang and beat out mesmerising samba rhythms which merged into a wall of carnival sound.

The Copacabbana stadium surrounded the beach volleyball court on all sides. On the court, battling for the World title were Karch Kiraly and his partner Pat Powers, veterans of the almost mythical 1984 Los Angeles indoor Gold medal USA team. They were jousting it out in forty five degrees with the current American beach gods Sinjin Smith and Randy Stocklos. It was the most incredible piece of television I had seen for many years and that simple twenty minutes hooked me for life. I no longer wanted to be an indoor player, I wanted to feel sand between my toes, to sip a cold beer with Randy, Sinjin and Karch court side in Rio. I wanted to be on the next available flight to Rio and to train for a year and compete in next years final. Fergus, equally enamoured of the whole scene also liked the plan. You will probably think I am mental. Looking back I think I was mental. Richard Callicott, E.V.A president at the time, was convinced I was mental when he fielded my phone call to him the very next morning.

I awoke at 8.00am, not a student hour, such was my mood after that early morning spiritual beach volleyball experience. I called by for Fergus, who had dressed himself appropriately in shorts a vest and flip flops, and we walked to the campus public phone box, in a freezing wind and pissing rain.

This is for real, but I actually called the E.V.A and demanded to speak to Richard Callicott. Our reason for being so bold was to contact the E.V.A and strike while the Transworld Sport iron was hot. Richard came on the phone. "I understand you have a proposal that you want me to hear ?" he said dryly. "Yes!" I replied, not even vaguely considering the notion that I may sound like a nineteen year old boy in a call box.

"I would like to know if the E.V.A would consider sending me and my friend Fergus to Rio to train for the year and enter next years World Championships."

There was a long pause. Richard was obviously very put out that an over excited youth with a plan so ridiculous, it would have made one of Baldrick's appear plausible, had been put through to his private office. He composed himself and finally dignified my enquiry with an answer.

"We receive an invite from the World Championship committee every year, to send a team to Rio. If you enter the English Beach Volleyball Tour and win it you will be eligible to represent England at those championships. I will put you back through to the secretary and if you give her your details she will send you an entry form." He said, very slowly and quietly and was gone.

I was almost speechless, we had a beach volleyball tour? I informed Fergus and we attempted to enter. It was in the days when Weymouth hosted the only real tournament and to get into that you had to be a division one NVL player, we were not and therefore we did not, get in that is. It was a highly competitive tournament, but completely innocent of the trappings of World beach volleyball. Players could enter a three person team, because everyone got so knackered that one of the team usually had cramp by 11.00am on the Saturday. The tournament ball was not a brightly coloured beach volleyball of the type we see today, but an indoor ball with Weymouth written on it. Early photos of the first few tournaments show that Polonia teams honoured volleyball tradition and played in their full indoor kit, including knee length red socks and trainers. Those players that decided to move on from indoor kit turned out in swimming trunks and huge aviator sunglasses, all fashionable at the time, very Magnum.

My interest did not fade in beach volleyball, but was temporarily diverted with dreams of indoor success and from there on in I was always too busy with training camps, to even entertain a trip to the beach. Although I still retained the notion that the beach was for me. When I did finally get to play though, the experience was so unlike my fantasy vision of success that once again my beach volleyball ardour was cooled. It turned out that beach volleyball was bloody hard work, sunburn, sand in places it should never be in and heat-stroke definitely didn't add to the mystique.

The Weymouth Beach Classic.
My sand career false start............

My first Weymouth experience was a tough lesson at the university of beach, majoring in 'sand is very difficult to play on'. Because I was a Capital City player, in division one, I was finally able to enter Weymouth. Neil Withington and Sean Poole, two team mates, agreed to play with me and following a Friday night England training session the three of us drove down to the south coast. I didn't drive at the time and as like many long time passengers I was blessed with a very strange concept of travel, known in psychological circles as 'completely no idea where I was going'.

Sean and Neil, two trusting souls, accepted my invitation to sleep at my parents house in Southampton. Southampton was, according to my distorted mental map, only a few miles from Weymouth, probably. It isn't only a few miles from Weymouth, Bournemouth yes, Chichester close (ish), but Weymouth, no, not in a month of Sundays. Parents door to Weymouth beach is a good hour and a half, with no traffic.

Nobody thought to check my calculations, they just trusted me. We set off for Southampton at about ten. Fifty miles down the M3 it occurred to me that I didn't actually have a clue how to get to my parents house, a disturbing piece of information which I really should have shared with the lads. However, Neil was looking tired and fed up and Sean is a big bloke. We ploughed on and in a bizarre act of blind faith Neil followed my confident sounding directions. Something he did on several occasions including the time when I was not concentrating on the M25 and we missed the M1 junction, difficult to believe I know, but we ended up doing two circuits of the London orbital at 1.30am in the morning with a journey to Leeds still to complete. Me looking sheepish and Neil mentally calculating is chances of getting away with the murder of an extremely annoying skinny ginger haired lad.

So it was under my expert guidance that we were now on the outskirts of Bournemouth, about forty five minutes from our intended destination. I bluffed on from there and at one in the morning we turned off the M27 towards my parents house. My Mum, who had also failed to question my travel arrangements probably just liking the idea of a rare visit from her son, woke us up at 6.30am so as she put it ' we could have breakfast and a shower, leaving just enough time to get to Weymouth to register at 8.30am'.

We sat at breakfast and the earlier gem of information began to register with Neil and Sean. It was now 7.00am and cramming toast into our mouths we sprinted out to the car. Neil drove us quickly along the roads towards Weymouth, overtaking caravans and weekend drivers that clutter the roads at that time in the morning. We drew closer to Weymouth and then suddenly on a long stretch of deserted single lane countryside road, Neil slammed on the breaks and we skidded to a halt.

Neil was transfixed, his gaze focused on a neighbouring field.

"What the hell is up ?" demanded Sean.

"Look" said Neil pointing frantically at a field full of hay bailed into cylindrical rolls, his face an absolute picture of amazement, eyes wide open.

"It's a load of those crop circles." he shouted. He was serious and that lightened the mood in the car........ a little.

We made Weymouth in record time and registered. Then sauntered down onto the sand. It had been years since any of us had been on to a sand beach, let alone done any training or for that matter ever played beach volleyball. We hit the sand and as do most people began that laboured sideways stagger that constitutes walking. The enormity of our task began to hit us and when we saw the local players warming up, in fact it damn near knocked us over.

The Weymouth rules excluded non division one players from the main draw. Strange really to let a bunch of Londoners with no concept of beach volleyball battle it our for the crown while confining the likes of Chris Eaton and Andy Cranstone, both Wessex players in division two, to the knock around 'B' tournament.

Chris and Andy, both superb beach players, consented to warm-up with us and play a scrimmage game to help us acclimatise. Our embarrassment at the apparent injustice of the division one rule was compounded when they beat us fifteen nil and I was completely unable to get a single ball over the net. Mind you, I forgot to mention in amongst all the other mishaps, I was playing with a fractured ankle such was my desperation not to be denied my beach volleyball chance once more.

Capital City, Me, Neil and Sean, did not win a single game. We were absolutely hopeless. The conversation I had had with Richard Callicott haunted me on every failed dive or shot into the net. Most of our orifices were filled with grating sand and it was a scorching hot weekend. The glamour had all but disappeared. By Sunday I was too burnt to carry on and the Copacabanna beach stadium seemed a very, very, very long way away, even allowing for my warped geographical perceptions.

I took a further two summers sabbatical from my pre-ordained career as a beach volleyball legend. Following the completion of the World Student games in 1991, I had a successful indoor season with Polonia and was now ready for another attempt at beach volleyball in the summer of 1992. All memories of my first effort had faded and that original Copacabbana vision began to invade my thoughts again.

The actual start to my beach volleyball career.
Neil Withington, 1992............

Neil Withington, now a Star Aquila player, had asked me to play the 1992 beach volleyball season with him. We got a good sponsorship with Sportset and I Dig volleywear and entered what was now an established set of tournaments. The tour was now called, rather ostentatiously, the Grand Prix. It was exciting to be part of and I had contributed directly to it's establishment when I was commissioned to draw the Grand Prix logo for the E.V.A.

The 1992 tour stopped at Margate, Weymouth, Bridlington and Bournemouth. It was an enjoyable season and generally we competed well, finishing a creditable fifth overall. The Grand Prix was won by the almost untouchable pairing of Rob Kittlety and Vince Joyce, Team O'neil surfwear.

The Polish dynasty.
Julian Banasiewicz, 1993 & 1994.....

By 1993 the tour had taken another step closer to becoming an almost semi-professional circuit. Dave Spears, the former England and Leeds player was ousted from his position as president of the beach commission by Andy Jones of W.H.White Poole and latterly Aquila. It was a shame because Dave had done so much for English beach volleyball from his base in Yorkshire of all places.

Within weeks Andy Jones had turned the presidency over to Ian Fairclough, one of the top players in the country. Ian was really committed to the game as a player and as a fan of the sport in general. Much has been said about his tenure with the beach commission, but improvements in the tour happened.

We were now due to play the 1993 season in Tenby, Isle-of-Wight, Bournemouth, Weymouth, Bridlington, Weston Super-Mare and Tynemouth (Newcastle upon Tyne).

My first three seasons in English beach volleyball were my most enjoyable from a social perspective. I finished fifth on the Grand Prix three times in a row, first with Neil then twice with my next partner Julian Banasiewicz.

The seasons were less pressured in terms of results, the players seemed o talk to each other more and the Saturday night was always good fun. In 1992, my first season, I began my chequered volleyball journalism career. I had already had cartoons published regularly in the E.V.A magazine and decided that I would start my own beach volleyball publication. At the Margate tournament 1992 the first 'Beach News' was launched. It was just a photocopied newsletter really, two A3 sheets folded, it went down a storm. Without fail, following it's launch, I was surrounded by players as soon as arrived at the tournament venue on the Saturday morning. I always sold out before the first games commenced. My fondest magazine memory was Weymouth of that year when play was suspended early on Saturday, due to thunderstorms. The players retired to the covered grandstand and most took out a copy or sat next to someone with a copy (tight bastards) of 'Beach News'. They laughed and shouted out various comments to each other, it was a very rewarding scene.

Beach News was occasionally factual and serious, but ninety nine per-cent humour and Mickey taking.

During the 1993 season the Weymouth committee, who used to host a Saturday night party in the local squash club bar, came to me with an idea. Graham Sawyer, Chris Brook and Steve Allgood, Grand Prix players them-selves, asked me if I would consider doing a 'Beach News' live act to get the evening going at the squash club. I agreed, god knows why, the smell of the greasepaint and all that I suppose. This meant that I spent the whole of the Saturday getting increasingly more nervous about the evenings enter-tainment. The act was basically a series of jokes at the expense of the play-ers and the E.V.A. I also did an impressions section. It was the type of impressions section where the impressionist is so bad that they precede every new impression by saying 'this is....' and then naming their victims.

The club was packed, it was touching as well as nerve racking that so many players had come to watch. I should not have been nervous because there was absolutely no way that the assembled players were going to let me die on stage. They were an incredibly friendly and pissed audience and laughed in all the right places, all in all it felt like a great experience.

I cannot really remember too much about the act. I know that I did an impression of Audrey Cooper and her use of her favourite cut shot. Mo Glover and her partner Mandy Kittlety and their south west accents also got a look in, you know the form. "I larffed and me mate larffed and we all larffed!"

I compared Chris Eaton with Steffi Graff and did a way over the top char-acterisation of Rob Kittlety and Vince Joyce and got away with it all. It was a good night. The person that got the biggest hammering though was Julian, my then partner. Or as Pat Powers likes to say. "My future ex-partner"

Julian is an austere sort of chap. He has a wonderful temperament and like all the polish players I have met he is generous and honourable to a fault. He also has a deep booming, slightly upper middle class accent and was one of the only impressions I could actually do convincingly. So I did it a lot. My favourite bit of the act was recounting what it was like to partner Julian. The funniest moments would usually come at training, down at Bournemouth beach.

When you train at Bournemouth you will always get a selection of pissed Scots, scousers, kids and foreigners come up to you and ask if they can play. Rather than let me go into a kind, polite, time wasting explanation of why that would not be possible, Julian would always stride past me and up to the enquiring party. It didn't matter who they were or how old they were, he had a fail-safe technique for putting them off. In his clipped almost military officer accent he would say (loudly).

"So you want to play then ?"

They would look at him, usually dumbfounded. Julian would speak again "Are you an international player ?" They would shake their heads.

"Right, well we are and you'd have to be that good to play us."

One hundred percent of the time they would walk away and ask no more questions.

The only time we got 'hoisted on our own petard', was an incident where we encountered a couple of beach volleyball bandits. Two small tanned lads came up to us and in very broken English asked if they could play. We were alone on our court, we had warmed up and had no idea whether some other players would be turning up to train. Julian still steamed in with the routine 'Are you internationals etc'. The pair shook their heads and retired to a safe distance. Julian and I continued to warm-up and hit balls over the net. The two lads were still there watching and no other players had shown up. In a strange change of policy Julian walked over to them and said in a voice clearly audible to the crowd gathered around the court.

"O.K! we'll play you, but it will cost you two pounds (cup of tea money for us), winner takes all."

We had won six pounds off a group of ten lads on a stag 'do' the previous weekend, they bet their money because they couldn't, as many don't believe that two could beat ten. Julian had obviously got a taste for the hustle. Our latest opponents nodded their agreement at the wager and came on to the court. They were hopeless and could barely play. So Julian went over to them again.

"I'm sorry." he said earnestly. "You're not very good at all, so it will cost you five pounds instead." The boys reluctantly agreed and after some very

160

poor hitting from them, we started the game.

Julian explained to them that we would have the serve and choice of ends, to give ourselves practice we decided to serve underarm and let them play at the good end, wind into their faces. The game began and the crowd had swelled following Julian's latest orations. I remember looking round the court, it surrounded with people on every line looking on intently while munching ice creams. Julian served underarm and I stood casually at the net wondering if the ball would come back at all. One of the players moved confidently in to position and took the pass while the other glided to the net, the pass technique was clearly grooved which woke me from my sloth. All of a sudden something was very wrong with the picture.

The ball hung above the net and the setting player leapt like a salmon, clean out of the deep Bournemouth sand and started to take a big left handed swing at the ball. I jumped and reached over the net, still a little confused at what was unfolding before me. The setting player looked at me and smiled, stopped his arm swing and set the ball out, no spin. I read the makers name on the ball as it floated away from me, we used to play with balls called Pro-Beach. The Pro-Beach logo was getting smaller and then, the ball was gone. The passer had moved to the net, jumped even higher than his mate and beat the living seagull shit out of the ball. He also put a bit of cut on the ball so it bounced off the sand, high in to the air and on to the promenade. The crowd went berserk and began to heckle us. I swear I heard someone say "Are you internationals?" in a false plummy accent.

Julian who had gone for the setting fake was stood on the opposite side of the court to the crater that had been left by the ball bouncing off the sand. To be honest we may as well have bent over and pulled our trousers down there and then. We tried to recover our composure and get in to the game, but we couldn't. We got absolutely raped, fifteen one in ten minutes flat.

Julian and I sportingly shook hands with the two, as it now emerged Brazilians, and asked if they would like to play another set. In suddenly much better English one of them sneered at us and said.

"No! give me your five pounds."

With that they took our money and wondered off along the beach laughing and joking, leaving Julian and I to face the delighted crowd. We never saw them again or found out who they were. I would like to think they were world class players, but such was the standard of English beach volleyball at the time, they were probably just kids having a knock about.

The following season 1994 was again fantastic. Beach News had lost none of it's popularity and now players were beginning to contribute ideas, jokes and photographs. Although that proved, on occasion, to be a difficult situation. On the one hand it was great to have contributors to the magazine on the other some of the material offered was unsuitable and had to be edited out, always risking offending the player who had submitted the story. The biggest problem was people's perceptions of what is funny and what level of Mickey taking at another players expense was acceptable. You have to follow a few rules when you are doing humour. With the male players it was far easier to blow up characatures and do wildly over the top pieces. You could also insult the players, providing it was funny. Most players seemed to enjoy seeing themselves featured. With the female players you had to be a little more careful, but they still enjoyed a good laugh at their own expense.

The problems arose when people submitted jokes or articles that were actually directly insulting, but they found their observations to be extremely funny. These contributors rarely employed subtlety in their writing and given their own way would have had me printing headlines like "Look at her, she's really fat" and "Nobody talks to him because he is boring and he smells." Not that clever and not really funny, but I suppose that is what an editor has to watch out for.

Julian and I were still in there scraping for results and at Bridlington we pulled off our best result to date beating the tour No.1 seeds Kittlety and Joyce, 15-9 on the Saturday, one of their only career defeats. We then lost to Cranstone and Eaton the No.2 seeds. In the Sunday rematch against Kittlety and Joyce we got knocked out, but finished with our second third place that season.

In the last tournament of that season we recorded our best finish ever and made our first beach volleyball final. The last tournament of that year was in Tynemouth, Newcastle Upon Tyne. It took all the players many hours to get up to the event.

Traditionally, the last beach tournament of the season usually acts as the venue for the indoor teams to secure top players for the coming campaign. Tynemouth was no different. The tournament had been weakened by Kittlety and Joyce heading off to an International tournament. This left Cranstone and Eaton as the No.1 seeds and Julian and I were seeded to meet them in the semi-final game on the Sunday.

We played well on the Saturday, with my Grandparents in the grandstands watching the games. My Nan with yet more packed lunch, always appreciated, and my Grandad unfortunately suffering from the early effects of Alzheimer's. They thoroughly enjoyed the day, my Grandad chatting to everyone and anyone. At one point getting us into a tricky situation when a rather over-weight spectator walked by and he accused her of trying to steal a beach volleyball by sticking it up the front of her T-shirt. He was always delighted to see me, mainly because he had forgotten that I was at the tournament since the last time I had talked to him, sometimes only minutes before.

The best bit of the day came when I joined them on the promenade after a match to find them engrossed in a game on the court furthest away from them. They were straining to watch four tiny dots on the horizon using opera glasses and clapping every time the play stopped. I asked them who they were watching and Nan turned round to me and told me she was watching her Grandson play. Then realising it was me she tapped my Grandad on the shoulder and said "Bob, that's not Simon playing, he's stood here." To which my Grandad turned his gaze from the court to me and said with delight on his face and for about the tenth time that day "Hello Simon, what a lovely surprise, what brings you up here then?"

The Saturday night served Julian and I with a huge slice of luck. Cranstone and Eaton, the hot favourites had agreed to play for Star Aquila. This agreement to play now constituted acceptance of the traditional Aquila right of passage into the team. Namely a heavy drinking session lead by the coach Phil Davies (Bear). The drinking games commenced in the hotel, watched by the non-Aquila players. Cranstone and Eaton were in the thick of it. They continued onto the Metro system and then into town. Reports circulated at breakfast that Chris Eaton had been sick on the Metro and Andy Cranstone had collapsed somewhere in a lift. By the time we began our warm-up to play them in the semi-final it was obvious the stories had not been exaggerated. They looked dreadful and were barely able to move. Needless to say mercy was not on the agenda and Julian and I beat them. It was the first of two passages to a final where I had far less to do with the result than outside forces.

We played badly in the final and lost 15-9 to Ian Fairclough and Ed Pearce, my first Grand Prix title chance gone and on the seven hour drive home it felt like it would be my only chance.

I had some really good times with Julian. He put up with all my bullshit and tantrums. He was mentally very consistent and attempted to curb my sometimes over zealous celebrations, in an effort to save me some slaps from bigger players. The problem was I was such a crap blocker that I made maybe one block per tournament. When I got my block I usually went mad. My shouting and jumping around never quite allied with Julian's preferred single shout of 'yes!' followed by concentrating on the next point.

I recall one situation when I blocked Rob Kittlety, I celebrated loudly and stared him down. Not a good idea. Julian jumped in and dragged me back from the net and said.

"Don't do that, you'll only antagonise him!"

163

I calmed down and returned to the net. Rob was pissed off at my shouting and decided to hit the next ball even harder. Absolute miracle, I got him again. This time there was no holding me and Rob had had enough. I noticed he was coming towards me and he didn't look happy. I could stay and fight. Rob is a six foot five, seventeen stone bouncer. This wouldn't have been a good call. I relied therefore on the thing that had often got me out of scrapes before, humour. I turned around and did a Monty Python style run away from Rob while doing the loudest high pitched scream I could. The crowd loved it and watched as Rob now laughing as well followed me across the court. The incident ended with Rob sportingly shaking my hand and as the crowd clapped he pulled me towards him and whispered, "do that again and I will break your legs".

Very faulty towers, the guest house option............

The English beach volleyball Grand Prix circuit is an enigma. It is a tremendous amount of fun to play on and is rich in characters and situations. The lack of any substantial funding from sponsors seems to have kept the tour friendly with a certain community spirit.

The lack of finance in the sport means that players are constantly on the look out for good accommodation deals as they travel around the country, in order to keep playing costs down. Paying less for accommodation naturally means guest houses and the English seaside guest house is another fantastically entertaining feature of the beach volleyball tour. Most places are friendly and genuinely interested in your welfare over the course of a weekend. Everyone though will have a guest house story and believe me I've heard a few. My personal favourite concerns a small establishment on the Isle-of-Wight when the tour used to stop at Sandown.

Freddie, my girlfriend, and I arrived at the guest house on the Friday evening around seven. We were greeted by a woman that was the spitting image of Dame Edna Everidge, but without the ostentatious clothing. She smiled at us politely and ushered us in to the hallway. Here we were instructed to stand on a 'rather nice rug that her son had brought back from Africa a few years earlier, it's real Zebra skin you know!' We dutifully stood as instructed and she treated us to a ten minute lecture on the do's and don'ts of her establishment.

To paraphrase her we couldn't shower before 10.00 am or after 3.00am. She would prefer it if guests didn't loiter around the place during the day, especially if they intended to shower presumably. Toilet paper evidently cost money and using it sparingly would be appreciated, over use identified by the tell tale whirring of the loo roll dispenser would be met by our hostess banging on the door and making loo paper related enquiries. Finally, if my girlfriend and I intended on 'cuddling up' at night, as she put it, would we kindly take it easy, our bed was comfortable, but as the rest of the guest house would testify at breakfast, it was noisy.

Lecture over we were honoured by being lead through to the inner sanctum to meet Les, her husband. "This is Les!" She proclaimed, pointing proudly at a large mass of motionless flesh on the sofa. "He won't get up to shake hands, he nearly died last year." She explained. For the duration of the weekend Les neither got up, nor spoke. There was in fact no discernible proof that Les hadn't actually died last year and our hostess was simply refusing to accept the fact.

Introductions over she fleeced us for our weekends rent money and took us up to the room. The room was a generous size, but walls were decorated in a violent lavender paint and the overall decor of the room could best be described as Laura Ashley on acid. In the middle of the room was a massive bed, which squeaked if you looked at it, let alone 'cuddled' on it. The lighting was ornate and our hostess took great pride in telling me that the light switches were a present from her son, who now lived in Australia. They were the kind of light switch that you could turn on and off and dim by clapping your hands. She also asked us to have a look at the door handles, another gift from Australia and apparently only made in that country. She pointed at some door handles which I had seen on thousands of guest house doors and I'm afraid I got the giggles. By the time she had shown us to the communal toilet and pointed to the hand painted sign that her son had commissioned for her, the tears were streaming down my cheeks. The sign read 'think before you pull the toilet roll, God wouldn't like you to take too much.'

That particular weekend was very enjoyable, despite the Happy Shopper value breakfast. She served Freddie with a steaming pile of various pieces of dead pig and we had to explain that Freddie was vegetarian. The plate was removed in stony silence and five minutes later, having obviously racked her brains for an alternative breakfast solution, she came back out to the dining room to offer Freddie some oxtail soup.

The worst guest house I ever stayed in was in Wales. I had decided to share a room with long time tour player, Gary Duncan. We arrived at the guest house Friday evening after a long and hideous drive through the rush hour traffic. On walking in to the hallway a stench hit us that made both Gary and I retch. Laying on the hallway floor like a great stuffed rug, was a huge spread of sandy brown animal hair. The only indication that it was

165

alive was the asthmatic wheezing noise and occasional rising and lowering of the hairy pile.

Gary, a medical sales rep, used to staying in far classier establishments rang the bell at reception. No one answered. Also used to far better service Gary rang the bell again. With still no apparent stirrings from the owners we began to get a little annoyed, the long journey contributing to our lack o good humour. Finally, a bored looking hostess emerged from a back room No hello, no welcome, just a curt "What do you want ?"

"We're booked in for tonight and tomorrow, Mr Golding and Mr Duncan' said Gary, barely able to contain his anger.

She checked the register, got us to sign in and gave us some keys. All in silence. The smell from what we assumed was a dog, was staggering. Gary had had enough. "Can you make sure the dog isn't there when I come down to breakfast tomorrow morning, I don't think I could stomach the smell." Gary said.

"Oh! she won't do you no harm." Came the reply from our hostess, who was looking lovingly at the massive ball of hair. "She's happy there, besides she can't move because of her arthritis, she's blind and deaf and can't breath very well because she weighs so much." She continued.

Gary was really fed up. "What do you call her ? Lucky!" He said and stomped off to the room.

Beach volleyball partnerships, should I stay or should I go now. Jurek Jankowski, 1995........

Most beach partnerships only last two years. Some will endure longer Kittlety and Joyce, Cooper and Glover and Wol and Gwinnett, Malone and Austin, but generally two years will do it. I could have played another year with Julian, but I think we both wanted a change and Julian was suffering with a calf injury. His injury gave me the opportunity to shop around and move on.

My choice of partner for the 1995 season turned out to be the wrong one. I asked Jurek Jankowski to play and genuinely felt that his remarkable volleyball ability was just waiting to be let loose on the sand. There was little doubt, even on the sand, Jurek is an amazing athlete. We got some good results but we should have been better. I had also made the mistake of taking on too much once again and I attempted to play the season while also coaching Mo and Audrey. It was a recipe for disaster. I went from the highs of the 1994 season as a player, to the as yet unrivalled honour of being asked by Audrey Cooper and Mo Glover to coach them on the World Series, to the most difficult lows I have ever suffered in volleyball.

First I quit my coaching job with Mo and Audrey in the June of 1995. Within weeks of the build up for the 1995 beach season with Jurek, cracks began to appear in the immature partnership. In hindsight he and I should have called it a day and what a day it could have been for me. Weeks out from the start of the season Grant Pursey arrived in England. I didn't know much about him, but he contacted me via the E.V.A and I collected him from the train station for his first English beach session at the lugubrious Ruislip Lido. Grant had just done a stint as coach of the Australian women's beach volleyball team and had spent time on the golden beaches of Brazil and South Africa. He was now in a car on a cold evening in England, heading towards Ruislip.

The lido is a clump of disgusting gritty orange sand, next to a mosquito infested lake in South West London. The look on Grant's face, when we drew up to the lido, said it all.

Jurek was busy for several weeks with exams, so I got to train as Grant's partner against a selection of the countries best teams. Playing alongside Grant is an incredible experience. I am sure like all of us he has his bad points as well, but none of those surfaced in the three weeks that we trained. Straight up, we won every single scrimmage set we played and I learned so much about the game from him.

There is something about Grant's consummate ability to read the game and decide on the perfect tactics that puts you at complete ease. Most of the things he said would happen in the games, did happen. When he called the shot all you had to do was hit it and it went down.

Then after three weeks a window of opportunity opened. Grant asked me if I knew of anyone he could play with. I did know a skinny ginger haired bloke and believe me I was tempted, but I just couldn't stitch Jurek up. We may not have been functioning well on and off the court, but Jurek is a good man and I just couldn't let him down.

Amongst many times when Jurek had looked out for me was the time that I came charging out of Polonia training at Ealing in 1992. I jumped into my van, a Bedford Rascal, to drive back home to Southampton. A journey I was doing there and back three times a week in a van that barely did more than fifty five miles an hour. I started the van, stuck it into reverse and shot backwards across the car park. I did not look in my mirror and next thing I knew there was a loud bang and I was slouched forward over the steering wheel. I had reversed up and over the bonnet of a black Peugeot and made a pretty atrocious mess. I put the van into first and drove off of the Peugeot trapped below. As the vans back wheels dropped down from the car, the tow bar caught on the Peugeot's front bumper and like the final comedic 'thud!' in a Laurel and Hardy 'car falls to bits scene', it ripped the bumper off.

What is one to do in those situations? I know about the insurance stuff and the law, but I mean the actual nitty gritty of confessing the act. There was no doubt in my mind that it was Jurek, my team Captain's car. With a heavy step, completely mortified at what I had done, I went back in to the sport centre. Jurek was still in the shower with most of the team, laughing and joking. The whole scene was macabre. I stood fully clothed in the shower and shouted over the water noise.

"Jurek!". There was no other way of saying it. "I've just smashed the front of your car in."

My problem in these situations is always the same. The 'crying wolf once too often' syndrome. I pleaded with him to believe me, but the more I pleaded the more he and the team laughed. Conceding that it was a good effort to wind them up. It was no good, I was going to have to go further. I ran, almost annoyed that he thought I was pulling his leg, back to the car park and Jurek's car. It was a bloody mess, worse than I remembered just minutes earlier. I picked up the whole front bumper from the floor and humped it back in to the sports centre. Jurek and the team were still in the shower laughing, clearly believing that I had been pulling their collective plonkers. I went into the shower this time with the bumper and held it up to Jurek. I felt like Jeremy Beadle putting the finishing touch to a spoof 'Oh no! we wrecked your car' sketch.

The team were finally silenced and they gazed on in morbid wonder as Jurek, lips moving, read the letters of his own number plate back to himself. With each letter it sunk in that I was actually telling the truth and the first proper car he had owned had been hideously assaulted by a middle hitter in a Bedford Rascal. Jurek's self control was phenomenal. He settled me down, realising I had a long drive ahead and point blank refused to take my insurance details. He gave me a cock and bull story about some work bonus he had received for doing up the car and would be covering all the repair costs himself. Enough said and we shall hear no more about this, shall we Simon. Now do you see my dilemma ? You can't dump a guy that has done that for you. So I recommended Grant contact Ian Fairclough and play with him.

I like to think I could have won something with Grant, although I am savvy enough to know he would not have stayed as my partner for more than a season. Grant likes to let me think that he would have agreed to play if I had asked him and I am happy to continue thinking that he might just have done so. In all honesty the 1995 season was not happy one for Jurek or myself. The only good thing to happen was that I got married in the August of that summer but not to Jurek.

In my partnership with Jurek I was equally the guilty party. We bickered, lost easy games and generally failed to get along in any aspect of the sport. It all came to a head in the last tournament we played, when I childishly turned up with only minutes to spare before a Sunday morning game against Grant and Ian, leaving Jurek to warm-up on centre court with his wife. During the game he absolutely let me have it and we went down 15-4, the partnership was mutually dissolved, with no need for either party to inform the other about their decision.

That is one of the key features in beach volleyball, one of the defining components that governs success or failure. Your partner and how you work as a team. You can win, but not get on all that well. Grant Pursey and Ian Fairclough are testament to that, but you have to be a massively strong character to survive.

In beach volleyball there is no hiding place. If you are playing badly or you have a problem with your partner you just can't get away from it, like you can in the indoor six-a-side game. It is an incredibly intense situation and the sun, the fatigue of matches and the crowd all contribute to the intensity. No matter how well suited you think you are or what great friends you thought you were, each partnership will have to deal with friction at some stage. Because, week in week out, the same behaviours will occur and the same mistakes will keep rearing their ugly heads until you just cannot keep a lid on it anymore.

Most teams deal with it effectively, even feed off it. Something Clayton Lucas my former beach partner and I learned to do during the 1999 season. Every so often though the lid will blow right off.

Without doubt that is the tough part of playing beach. You have to want to play for your partner as well as your self. If you don't feel like playing, the sand can start to become very deep indeed. Many players choose to play with people they know or they are friendly with. This can be a bad decision. Once the pressure is on and results begin to matter you will see a different side to your partner. Some get aggressive, some get moody. Everyone will have some sort of indiosynchratic reaction to the stress of training and more so, to competition. It is sometimes hard to remember that on court personas rarely reflect the real partner. It is like someone you thought you knew growing horns and a little pointy tail. If you have had a tough day on the courts it can take time for your partners new body parts to fade from sight.

You will always share something with your former beach partners, especially if you have achieved some good results. But, when the time comes to split and move on, that is when things get tough.

There are very few mutual partnership break ups in beach volleyball, yet most are presented to the outside world as just that. The break up details usually remain between the parties involved. It is kind of an unwritten rule I suppose, but you rarely hear about who dumped who, why and how. It can be so like a couple breaking up.

There is no precedent or standardised format for dissolving a beach partnership. It is common place on the A.V.P (Association of Volleyball Professionals) in the States, part and parcel of professional volleyball. Players constantly assess their current standings and very often choose to move to a partner that they feel will help them to win. The professional tour in the states is brutal. The shorter players, great athletes in their own right working so hard to win on the tour, are often victims. Jim Nichols, one of the shortest players to ever play professional beach volleyball, 5 foot 7 inches, remembers his tough breaks vividly.

If a team gets a good result it can be just as difficult to hold onto a partner as when you get a bad result. Nichols, a defensive player like myself, is totally reliant on big blockers to make his game work. If a tournament went well he could pretty much guarantee others would attribute the success to his much bigger partner and be straight on the phone trying to lure them away. They usually went.

Nichols recalls his best ever AVP result, a fourth with Jose Loiola. Loiola, a lunatic high jumping, hard hitting Brazilian now ranked in the top three in the World, was just off the plane and had nobody to play with. Nichols had just been dumped so he agreed to play with the Brazilian bomber. They got fourth and all looked well. Nichols flew home and got back to his apartment to find his answerphone flashing. "Hi! Jim....Jose.....I not play no more."

Even in the States, after thirty seasons of beach volleyball, players still do whatever they can to avoid a face to face showdown.

The most famous pairing on the beach, aside from Karch Kiraly and Kent Steffes, were Sinjin Smith and Randy Stoklos. They played together from 1988 to 1994 winning several World Championships and hundreds of AVP titles, both making over a million dollars each from the partnership. It was a sensation when they split and Randy Stocklos moved to play with Adam Johnson. Even more sensational was Randy's decision to dump his long-time partner also taking the time honoured answerphone option. They were more than a team. They were friends and Randy was a house guest of

Sinjin's for many years, so they were close. In the end Randy reputedly rang when he knew Sinjin was away and left his message. I would have paid money to get a listen to that tape.

In my eight seasons on the domestic tour there has been a dramatic change in the way players function. In 1992 players stuck together, they were a team and more often than not they were mates, severely testing their friendship bond. Now players are starting to function as individual entities making partner decisions based on what is best for them. Most of the top players now have 'histories' shall we say. You can practically guarantee that you will encounter a former partner during tournament play. These, believe me when I tell you, are the best games to watch. It's almost worth producing a who's who of beach just to chart your spectating for the day.

In the 2000 season I had the opportunity to run into three ex's still competing at the top, hmmm! great. Back in 1996, Margate, I had my first ever match against an ex. It was an amazing game against Jurek Jankowski and Stuart Watson. Mine and Jurek's previous disastrous season was still very much an issue. I was partnering Steve Draper and it was the last game on Saturday, the loser would go out. Jurek and I were focused on putting one over on each other. Steve was at his snarling, aggressive best and Stuart just tends to hate everybody and everything when he is on court. The teams abused each other to thirteen points a piece, Steve and I finally turned them over fifteen thirteen. Jurek and I did not shake hands and words were exchanged, while Steve and Stuart like two big sides of very angry beef, went chest to chest in an awesome pose off. The crowd loved it.

The Draper years, 1996 & 1997..............

My partnership with Steve was a turning point in my beach volleyball career. We teamed up in 1996 and played two seasons together. It was the first real opportunity I had to be really competitive on the tour. Steve is a huge player at the net and I switched from my previous blocking role to a defensive one. Like anything it took time to learn to defend and to learn to play with Steve. We had an indifferent start, but as the season progressed results began to come.

Over our two years as a team we gained a 'nearly men' tag. We lost 17-16 to Grant Pursey and his new partner Chris Eaton at the Cleethorpes Grand Prix. Then in a televised game at the British Championships in Battersea Park we lost 17-16 to Danny Wol and Greg Gwinnett from 13 - 10 up. Greg and Danny eventually went on to take the British Title in that tournament.

The biggest 'nearly' occurred at the Weston Super-Mare Grand Prix in 1996. It was the last event of the year and Grant and Ian were away on International duty, leaving the rest of us to compete in a bun fight for the final. Steve and I had an extremely fortuitous passage to the final. We scraped it out on Saturday going through to the winners final play off for a spot in the Grand Prix final. It was mine and Steve's first straight winning day on a Saturday and the evening soiree had never felt so good. We were drawn to play Tim Hollis and Marek Banasiewicz in the winners final.

Tim and Marek had just returned from a ninth place finish at a World Series qualifier event, the best ever finish by a British male team. They had even recorded a win over a seeded Russian team. Steve and I showed up early for the match, scheduled as a 9.00am start. We warmed up well and began to notice that neither Marek or Tim were present. Tim eventually turned up and began his warm-up, but still no Marek. Neither Steve or myself had ever been to a final. We were truly psyched for the game. Time passed and with no Marek the referee began the countdown to award the match to us. Tim retired to the stands having decided his partner was not going to show. I remember looking over to him in the stand, it was unsettling, he looked like the loneliest guy on the beach. If Marek had shown up then I think mine and Steve's heads may not have been on the game.

Marek didn't show. The referee blew the whistle and Steve and I, unsportingly, celebrated our place in the final. We finished our celebrations and calmed down enough sign the score sheet and shake hands and apologise to Tim. We turned around from doing that and stood behind us with his kit bag, looking incredibly confused was Marek, just showing up for a 9.30am warm-up. The disputes raged on while Steve and I left for the cafe to celebrate our 'win?'

That then was my second lucky route into a final, a final that was very difficult to settle in to. Our opponents Greg and Danny had already appeared in a couple of finals, so the experience was not as new to them as it was to us. In the first set we just froze and went down 15-3. All the way through I just kept saying to Steve, think about the next set, we can do it then. It was in the days when the finalist who had struggled through the losers bracket to the final would have to beat the winning finalists twice, to gain the title. The second set was to seven points and Steve and I were in the final from the winners bracket. The tournament systems in those days were more complicated than a trying to understand a tax rebate form.

We settled down for the second set. Danny and Greg could not maintain their pressure and Steve and I lead all the way. At 6-5 up Steve hit a great serve, Greg set Danny way off the net and maybe the ball was spinning a little. We kept our focus though and Steve made a great defensive play, digging Danny's spike to the net. I ran in to make the set and this is where I suddenly and completely understood the need for experience in sport.

It was a situation I had never been in before. I had a great pass, right on my head and all I needed to do was set the ball for Steve to finish. Just like I had done a thousand times in practice. Danny and Greg had even backed off, it was a free hit. The difference was, it was all on tournament point. All of a sudden everything slowed down. My arms and legs felt heavy and I found myself thinking through scenarios of a double touch on the set or setting Steve to far away from the net. I set the ball, it was clean. But I had overcompensated in my efforts to give Steve the perfect hitting opportunity. The ball stayed completely in line with my shoulders and headed towards the net. Steve jumped really high and swung, he missed the underside of the ball. The ball went over the net and dropped in front of a wrong footed Danny in defence. Steve and I went berserk in celebration. Danny and Greg moved to shake hands with each other, no protest, nothing. Just an acceptance of their defeat.

Cutting through the cheers and celebrations came a shrill whistle. The referee was blowing and gesturing with his hand over the net. The referee had called that the ball had passed untouched over the net, not square to my shoulders. A fault. On the biggest point either of us had ever played, the referee made a really big call. Steve and I turned from celebration to protest, we went absolutely crazy at the referee. We felt we had won the game fair and square and all but the referee seemed to agree. Naturally the referee stuck to his decision. We called a time-out. I thought we had sorted ourselves out mentally. We sided out and I had a chance to serve for the game. I hit the ball way out over the baseline, but really it was all over. Danny and Greg calmly took the next two points to win the title 7-6. We were devastated and I was pretty emotional. It took us hours to come out from under the umbrella shading our players court side seating and if I hadn't had to drive back for a gig with my band I would have stayed there until I was forcibly removed.

You never forget things like that, but the more you experience them the more you can learn. It's so important to learn positively about yourself and your partner in those situations. Learning from those situations will enable you to continue and develop as players. Steve and I are both hot headed. We would both shout when we felt situations were going against us. Sometimes it worked for us and sometimes not. In that situation it cost us.

Most teams will have a story of when they played Steve and I and we began to growl. We salvaged many results by switching on the aggression. If we lost though it was not a pretty sight. We found it difficult to switch off.

Ginger, mean, argument machine.
When the red mist descends..............

Indoors I had already developed a reputation as a bad loser, an aggressive player and someone not afraid of telling referees what I thought. I am not proud of that, it is just the way it was. When I see other players behaving badly it always looks so ugly. But, on the other hand I can understand what is going on in that players head. When I got mad at College Nick or Simon would bench me. At Capital City Sava would send me to Coventry, well Prague in his case. It all contributed towards my learning what was unacceptable behaviour. By 1994 I was supposedly grown up and should have been able to control my outbursts, but they still used to occur. I will always be eternally grateful to players and referees who have encountered my temper as it was and have dealt with me intelligently, both warning me and helping me. Possibly remembering occasions in sport where they have found it tough to control their own tempers.

My temper meant I tried it on with refs, on occasion I did some pretty radical things to try to win, as Graeme Sawyer the Weymouth organiser and former beach player will testify. In 1992 playing with Neil against Graeme Sawyer and Steve Harrison we were 14-13 down and the ball had been shanked by Neil and was heading under the net, we would have gone out of the tournament. Because the centre line does not exist on a beach court you can technically go underneath the net and play the ball back under again and into your court, providing you don't interfere with a player in the opposition court! That conjures up a picture doesn't it. I dived full tilt, I was never going to get anywhere near the ball, I knew that so I dived into Graeme and hit him square in the stomach. Interfere with him, I damned near committed indecent assualt on the poor bloke. We both hit the sand and I was straight up and over to the ref claiming I could have played the ball and he (Graeme) had stopped me from doing so. The uncertain ref, a clueless player (ring any bells, referees out there?), gave the decision to me and Neil and we played on and won. Five minutes after the game I was absolutely racked with embarrassed guilt, Neil didn't speak to me for a while. Graeme, always the gentleman reasoned with me about the incident, but did not attempt to take any reprisals and stood by the refs decision.

The other person I shall remain eternally grateful to is Stuart Dunne, the referee, a referee the players have really come to respect and trust over the years. In 1993 I had just hit a shot while playing for England Civil Service against Scotland Civil Service in the National Championships. The shot was, as it happened, the last of the game and we lost a very aggressive game 2-1, 17-15 in the last set. I had hit the ball down the line, it caught the blockers arm and went out, I and my team assumed we were still in the game against a very strong Scottish team. The ball had brushed the blockers arm at high speed, right under Stuart's nose, it was impossible for him to see the touch and the blocker was now openly celebrating and indicating subtley that he had touched the ball Ha! Ha! etc. He was never going to admit the touch in a month of Sundays. I was openly abusive to Stuart. I finally went over to the score table, thinking I had calmed down and would be able to shake Stuart's hand. I took his hand and a wave of frustrated anger hit me again and while shaking his hand I found myself once again shouting at him. Stuart had dealt with the situation brilliantly, but couldn't take anymore of my crap. We were after all supposed to be friends, some friend I was. He increased the pressure on my hand and dragged me towards him. "I don't have to take this, Simon! Just shut up!" he said very quietly, but forcefully to me.

I went mad again and this time we ended up, still holding hands, in a physical tussle which resulted in us falling onto the scorer's table. It was a nasty incident and Stuart could have got me banned, he would have been completely within his rights. For whatever reason, he didn't and I escaped sanction. I was mortified by what I had done and said. Days later I rang Stuart, not because I was worried about official reprisals, but because I genuinely wanted to apologise, I desperately needed to apologise. Stuart accepted my apology graciously and I learnt a very valuable lesson. Namely, that wherever humanly possible I have to try to curb my outbursts and my game will benefit from a better focus and fewer episodes of guilt and worry. But it still doesn't stop the occasional relapse.

At Bournemouth, earlier in the 1996 season I was involved in my worst display of temperament on the beach. Something that I am able to laugh at now, mainly because the referee concerned has forgiven me, but in retrospect it concerned me greatly. Steve and I were 14-9 up against Paul Curtis and Gary Joyce a team that is renowned for their noise and chat on court. Their confidence and energy on court makes them one of the most difficult teams to get past in the draw. The game was a predictably touchy affair. We got the upper hand, then really tightened up at the same time as Gary and Paul began to battle their way back. Losers to go out of the tournament. They got to back 15-14 up. Paul picked up a shot from me and dug it to Gary. Gary was setting for the matchpoint hit. He mishandled the ball. It caught in his hands and span out, no more than two feet above his head. Let's face it, nobody deliberately sets two feet above their head on the beach. Steve and I turned to each other and celebrated being let off the hook. The referee didn't blow the fault so Paul Curtis, realising quickly that that the ball was still in play, dived towards Gary and hooked the ball from just off the sand, up and over our heads for the point. Game to them.

I couldn't contain my anger and went completely mad at the referee. He dealt with the situation well and refused to become involved with my demented ranting even Steve, master ranter, stepped in to try to calm me down. I was shouting and swearing about the ref's credentials, or lack of them. Even Paul and Gary tried to calm me down. I finished my attack by shouting, "That sponsored gear you're wearing, take it off and put it in a bag and give it back to the organisers. The only way you should be wearing it is if you go and buy it from a shop."

Quite a crowd had built up now. There was a brief silence as my shouting abated. Then, emerging from the crowd, came the referee's wife. She had quite rightly had enough of me and I am glad she had, at least some of the status quo was restored and I no longer looked the complete bastard that I had seconds earlier.

"You evil, horrible man." She screamed. "Who the hell do you think you are, your language is disgusting, you should be banned from the Grand Prix forever."

It was like a cold wet slap in the face. It brought me back to reality and calmed me down. I walked away from the court. Again no action was taken against me. It is true the referee's decision was wrong and months later when we talked he said he knew that. But I had no justification, for my level of behaviour. Another learning experience I guess. I always watch other players losing it and it just looks so funny most of the time. In the players tent next to centre court this season I and several other players had some excellent disagreements with the refs, all greeted with howls of derision from the players. You know after one of those centre court bust ups the other players will give you a tough time. From then on you won't be able to walk into the tent without someone repeating your finest line "No, No, you be quiet and listen, that ball hit the aerial and was out and you know it and they know it. Go on ask them, go on!" My particular best effort of the 2000 season.

It was a strange transition to have referees join the tour. No players like to referee, so we have all enjoyed the referees taking that duty away from us. The players refereeing caused some hideous disputes and tension. Few player referees were ever strong enough to make the tough decisions and then apply the letter of the law. I have been abused badly on several occasions most notably by Clayton Lucas and by Richard Dobell. As a player you know the score and the competitors will tend to apologise when they calm down.

Only Andy 'mushy' Jones ever took the refereeing duties all the way.

Greg Gwinnett, early on in a Saturday match disputed one of Andy's calls and called him an obscene name, Andy sent him off. The insuing argument was a real treat to watch.

Therein lies the rub. Fair play, honesty and on court respect will give you a great feeling inside. It's a sporting ethos that has been preached over many generations and can be wonderful to watch. Going head to head in pressured sports contests produces great moments. The fact remains, that a great bust up, some snarling and a belting disagreement with the referee, may not be everyone's 'cup of isotonic drink', but it certainly appeals to me. I'm not the only one either, just look at the popularity of WWF wrestling, fights in rugby and ice hockey and the fascination with chracters like John McKenroe.

Without doubt, from all the volleyball head to heads I have watched and been involved in, one emerges as my all time favourite. There was no hint of the 'feel good factor' in this game, just good old fashioned kill or be killed. In the Bournemouth Grand Prix 1997 the infamous Gable twins had made it to the final. The Gable twins were a couple of Californian media darlings with dual passports and had come to play on the English Grand Prix and to carry the 'English flag' on the World Series. Their behaviour and general manner put them at odds with most of the domestic tour. Whatever you thought of the Gable's though, their addition to the tour certainly spiced things up.

Steve and Darren, or Gabe and Deek as they called themselves on court, started on the wrong foot. This was probably a media ploy, but boy did it stir things up. They had slagged off the Grand Prix Tour and it's players in the press, then gone back to the American press and claimed they were both the founding father's and leading lights of British beach volleyball. True they were good, on their day. They were not however, the World Series and Olympic contenders they tried to make us believe they were. Their crash and burn results on the World tour confirmed that. On the Grand Prix they never really won games convincingly. The tournaments they won and the top teams they beat were only ever achieved by the narrowest of margins. They were turned over too many times to be taken seriously, notably by Kittlety and Joyce at Cleethorpes and extremely enjoyably 15-4 beating by Danny and Greg at the British Championships.

My own opinion of the Gable team is tainted I will admit. I played them once on the tour, with Clayton. In the warm-up a twin threw my ball in the sea, I threw a hand full of sand, with a stone in it, at his groin. The stone hit him and he whinged. Then in the game we put the pressure on and got to

10-10. They started to shout stuff. Following a big hit which I failed to defend with my shoulder, they enquired did I need a medical time out. That was it then, we were going to shout back. "Can you feel it!" shouted Clayton after a huge roof block, complete with obscene actions.

"You can't say that on the World Series man!" replied one of the beach style batty boy twins.

"Is that the World Series where you keep getting shafted." Intelligent, moral high ground taken by myself in response.

So it continued. Then at 10 -10 on the switch of ends one of the twins kicked me in the leg. He lost his cool and just belted me in the shin, with a frustrated 'small boy not getting his own way' look on his face. I was not happy and alerted the referee, who had seen nothing so naturally did nothing. I could have gone down, thrown myself on the sand, taken a dive premiership style, and stayed down screaming and rolling around to get a decision. I'm still glad I didn't. So my view is definitely tainted. But in my view, for what it is worth, the Gable twins were both completely full of shit.

Back to the 1997 Bournemouth Final, with everyone staying in the drizzle to watch what looked like it was going to be a cracking final. The Gable's opponents and probably their harshest critics were Grant Pursey and Chris Eaton.

Both teams played brilliantly. The through the net interplay and posturing was something to watch and enjoy. Grant was at his best and Chris supported with some strong blocking and big hits. The game could have gone either way. In my humble opinion though, on play, Grant and Chris should have edged it. The Gable's were gutsy bastards though. The whole game revolved on a disgraceful, yet fascinating incident. Grant had attempted a shot and cut the ball down on to the sand. He had fallen over after the off balance shot and was laying prostrate, next to the net. Grant celebrated the point from his position on the floor. The Gable twin blocking did not like it and his little 'kicking' problem resurfaced. Clearly and in front of hundreds of witnesses he kicked Grant.

He kicked Grant and 'it' kicked off. The crowd was shouting, Grant and Chris were face to face with their petulant opponents at the net and the referees jumped in to sort it out. Chris was shouting.

"Forget the volleyball, you and us lets go, right here right now." He meant it and when Chris means it, you don't argue.

Calm was eventually restored and unbelievably no action was taken against the assailant. It was blatant, everyone saw, but still nothing. The injustice seemed to get to Grant and Chris. They played hard but just lost out on the last point of the third set. When the Gables put the last hit down they went crazy and very pointedly an unsportingly ran over to Chris and Grant's girlfriends to lord their win. It was completely unacceptable behaviour. It was however, the sort of match about which you could justifiably say, 'I was there.' Grant's girlfriend got some revenge. Mel and some of her friends wrote to the American Volleyball magazine and they printed her harshly worded criticism of the Gables and set the record straight on a few pieces of misinformation fed to the press by the Californian boys. The letter was printed unedited, it turned out that the Gables didn't enjoy that much popularity across the pond either.

Lucas opens a can of 'Whoop-Ass', 1998 & 1999

In 1998 I decided to team up with Clayton Lucas.   In that season and 1999 I had to play against Steve, now my former partner, at Weymouth and then Tenby respectively. I was playing some good volleyball with Clayton Lucas, no wall flower himself. In 1998 Steve lost out, but by 1999 he had teamed with Stuart Watson. That team should be illegal, two six foot four plus psycho monsters on one court.

We met them twice in the 1999 Tenby tournament. Game one on the Saturday Steve and Stuart beat us 16-14, last game of the day. Steve got to lay a couple of ghosts and celebrated quite rightly. It was a tough loss for me. On Sunday it could not have been organised better. Clayton and I to play Steve and Stuart for third place overall, centre court. The game was almost a carbon copy of the one the previous evening. Both teams ground it out, but as the points mounted, began to snarl it out. It came down to some classic one-upmanship with all four players giving it large after every kill or defensive play.

Steve and Stuart threw the kitchen sink at me on serve. With Clayton's fantastic setting I managed to hang in and keep my sometimes fragile sideout game together. The turning point came when Steve unloaded a real bomb down the line at me on a free hit. I managed to dig him overhand and roll a winner short over the net, then admittedly went through the net on the celebration. This seemed to quiet the match and we nicked the game fifteen thirteen.

There were several reasons for my change of partner, the main one being that I had long admired Clayton's ability on the sand and was convinced of his potential. We kicked off the partnership with a 16-14 loss to Grant and Chris in an invitational exhibition match, then followed it up with a 15-10 win over them in the Brighton Top Eight tournament. It was a dream start for us as a team. Then with the pressure on in the first three tournaments of the season we crashed and burned with consecutive fifth places. This we responded to with a lot of hard work in training, trying to get our game together. So often beach volleyball seasons come down to one or two key matches. Win them and your seedings will be secure, lose and you will have some really tough Saturdays. At Margate, a tournament we nearly pulled out of because of injury, we found ourselves in a season crunch game, last thing that day.

We had fought through two tough games previously but were in reasonable shape for the third game. It was the first time we had not encountered Grant and Chris, we got a chance to have a go at Steve Fee and Tim Hollis, the number two seeds. Playing with Clayton added a new dimension to my game. Those of you that have seen him play will know he can jump. I remember watching the Whitfield final in 1998 sat next to Gary Duncan. We spent the warm-up and most of the game just marvelling at Clayton, shoulders and head above the net and perfectly balanced in the air, cranking the ball. His ability to jump and stay balanced meant that defending behind his block was mostly a breeze.

The other factor was his speed around the court. He is a quick and brave defender. These combined attributes made us a tough team to beat, this won us a lot of games and respect. Our best performances came when we were bouncing around court and off each other, making tough plays and shouting. There was usually a fair bit of shouting, mostly at the opposition and sometimes at each other. When we got fired up though, we felt we could play against anyone on the tour.

In the crunch game against Steve and Tim, they galloped to a lead and then found themselves in the classic position of 14-9 up and suddenly, inexplicably unable to finish the job off. A common sporting problem. Clayton has a good eye for a fight. He and Anthony Roberts pulled off the most incredible comeback ever on the Grand Prix tour, from 14-0 down they came through to beat Dave Ryvers and Martin Curtis 16-14 in 1995.

We must have looked out of it, but we certainly did not feel that way. The comeback started when I made two huge pick ups off of hard driven balls by Steve. The first was legitimate, but the second hit me in the neck. I was in the right place, but I really didn't know much about it. That was the catalyst we were looking for and Clayton took over comeback duties from there. He got another couple of inches on his jump with pure aggression and began to block everything. Steve and Tim very kindly got tighter and tighter. The last two points were vintage Clayton. He began to talk to Tim through the net saying that he was probably going to block him, but volunteering this information in a very matter of fact tone. At 15-15 Clayton did what it said on the tin and pulled off two huge late blocks. On the second with the realisation that we were the winners we celebrated good and proper.

This win was indeed crucial and we ended up against Gary Duncan and Anthony Roberts in the semi-final. Not an easy game by any means, with Anthony being Clayton's ex partner. It was just one of those weekends though and we had another good game against them to make our first Grand Prix final and turn the season around. We went on to finish third overall that year. The season ended on a high note when we beat Danny and Greg in the final of a televised invitational event in London, 12-2 and 12-6. Not a Grand Prix win, but at least I had won something.

The 1999 season was difficult. Year two in a partnership always throws up the mental challenges. Clayton was working really hard and had almost no opportunity to train. He was also preparing to become a father. I was in the process of long exhausting interviews for promotion at work and the consequence of this pressure was that Clayton and I were bitching at each other more and more. The other factor was that for me it was my best season so far, for Clayton who had previously won the British title with Richard Dobell, it was not quite the same.

We still got some great results, but my injuries were starting to catch up on me. My torn cartilage in my right knee was causing serious problems and by game three on Saturday I was usually struggling. Despite that we made two finals and finished third at three tournaments.

The last tournament of the 1999 season was Weymouth, the English beach volleyball Mecca. Relatively few players have made the legendary Weymouth final. Clayton and I knocked off Danny and Greg 15-6 in the semi and achieved what was for me one of the high points of my playing career. A final in front of a big crowd in the oldest beach tournament in the country, the tournament where it all started for me.

In the final we decided to serve Grant exclusively and try to wear him down, be patient and take the game at the last. It was a very hot day with no wind and the plan was good. Unfortunately it relied on two vital elements. The first was my ability to keep going considering that Grant, if served constantly, was gong to serve me all day long in return. An eye for an eye. The second factor was that we had to control our tempers in the early phases of the game when Tim and Grant are more than capable of tearing teams to bits. The second factor proved to be the main problem, although it kind of worked in our favour.

Two weeks prior to the tournament Grant and Tim had thrashed us 15-0 in the Margate final. A very humbling and frankly unpleasant experience. They served me off court. We now found ourselves on court at Weymouth, Grant doing what the hell he wanted on side out and 6-0 down. This meant twenty one unanswered points to them. Clayton called a time-out. We sat solemn under the sun shade sipping our water. The tension was ridiculous and Clayton decided it was time to employ his fail-safe method for cheering things up, squirt me with water. He drenched my shorts and made a throwaway remark. I completely lost it and began to shout at him. We ended up in the most massive row hurling abuse at each other. The referees made their way over to calm things down, by which time we were up to full steam. The abuse continued to some shoving and at that point the referee warned us that if we kept going he would eject us from the game.

We finally stopped shouting. Grant and Tim were transfixed, both peeping out from below their sun shade at the bizarre scene. Clayton and I went back to court, in the middle of court it kicked off again, then as suddenly as it had begun Clayton diffused the whole thing. He gave me a massive hug, right in the middle of centre court in front of all those people. As he grabbed me he whispered,

"Right! are we going to play now?"

The effect was magnificent. We were so fired up and in addition Grant and Tim had completely lost their focus.

Clayton pulled off the most fantastic blocks I have ever seen for our first point. He jumped and roofed Grant straight down, one handed reaching right inside and over the net. Just brilliant. After that block we scored eight more points for a 9-6 lead. I missed a swing for 10-6, just out over the side line and that gave Tim and Grant a chance to recover. We stayed out a very long time in that game, but eventually went down emotionally and physically drained 15-10. Crucially for us with some pride restored.

Over the winter Clayton decided to make the break. A good decision for him and one that we had talked about. The best option was for Clayton was to team up with Scottish player Morph Bowes the former Belgian professional and current Great Britain international. This makes a team that a lot of people will want to watch and not want to play against. Despite being privy to this whole concept it was still difficult when Clayton finally made his decision known to me. I had played quite a few matches with him and we had been a successful team making four finals in two years on a competitive tour. My main worry was that for me it was all over.

Sitting on the consultants bench in December, with a confirmed torn cartilage and no beach partner, I was feeling worse than I had ever felt in my sporting career. I thought I could accept it and retire gracefully, but I'd never done anything gracefully up to that point and I didn't feel like I wanted to start then.

My Mum has always spoken about the fact that I do seem to have a tremendous amount of luck in my life. I suppose on reflection I do have an unusual knack of being in the right place at the right time. She prefers 'if you fell down the toilet you would come up smelling of roses', but it equates to the same thing in the long run. Once again this season my cup runneth over. No partner, struggling for fitness and to be honest getting pretty uninterested in playing on. Living in a small town in the New Forest, not exactly the hub of World beach volleyball and with no prospect of a player available for duty, I was up a creek without a proverbial paddle. Then Grant, who works at the same College as me, ambles in to my office in March. "Simon, you thinking of playing this year ?" he asked.

"Oh I don't know, I can't find anyone to play. Nobody seems interested in teaming up with an ageing kneebophobic (that is a legitimate phobia by the way, look it up) I probably won't play." I whinged back.

"Shame!" said Grant nonchalantly, "Cos' there's an Australian world series player moved to the New Forest, he's looking for a partner and I put in a good word for you." You see what I mean, about my Mum being right. It is amazing how quickly knee pain can evaporate with the right treatment and the offer of a chance to team up with a dirty great world sries monster. I sit on my rapidly expanding, lazy arse giving it 'woe is me' and naturally I get my reward.

Inspired by the possibility of another season, I was advised by a friend to visit a very good physiotherapist. I guy called Adrian Schooter, based near Brighton and former head Physio to the Brisbane Bulls Rugby league squad. It was a last throw of the dice really. I limped into his office and he began to examine me. He was brilliant, carefully discussing symptoms and then thoroughly examining the knee. He confirmed that I had a torn cartilage and showed me exactly where it was, but then told me the knee pain and general lack of mobility was down to the fact that my medial quadriceps muscle had, as he put it, gone on a holiday.

The medial quad or teardrop as it is referred to by body builders, is the muscle that is situated just above the kneecap and on the inside front of the leg. Mine was completely wasted and I don't mean drunk. It was almost non-existent due to the injury causing me not to use my right leg. The medial quad controls the last ten percent of the leg movement when straightening the leg. So Adrian, using all the high tech options at his disposal, sent me home with instructions to duck tape a house brick to a training shoe and sit and do hundreds of repetitions contracting my medial quad through only the last ten percent of the leg extending movement. He said that if I did this I could probably get two more summers, before an operation and retirement. So I went away and did what he said. I worked harder on my leg than I had worked on any part of my training for sometime, because there now seemed to be a purpose.

By the end of May, Adrian's diagnosis proved to be correct, the knee pain was going and my leg was getting stronger and stronger. I was even able to begin to play on the sand.

From Bondi to Barry Island. Tristan Boyd, 2000.........

I was now able to face the first few sessions with my prospective partner, Tristan Boyd. The fact that he was a former Australian World Series player added a touch of frisson to the usual first training session. His call a week before training had taken some of the pressure away.

"Yeh, Hello is that Simon? I hear you're the only player left!" He said and didn't laugh.

The first training session with a new partner is another beach phenomenon. You turn up all smiles and jokes, you train all apologies for mistakes. 'No please that was definitely my fault!' You ask questions, where do you want me to set the ball for your hit ? Where shall I stand on court ? What calls do you do? But everything usually changes and most teams will argue at some stage. It always reminds me of the old poem about how a couple interact with each other over time. As a courting couple the young lady trips over her own feet, her young man catches her as she falls and says "There, there my dear, is everything alright?" He inquires. By the time many years have passed and the lady once again trips over her feet, her man, now her husband lets her fall. "Oh! pick your feet up you silly cow!" He says angrily.

The whole session is one big try out. It feels usually very awkward, it is never easy to just go on court and play with another player. With Tristan though, as with Clayton and Grant before him, it was relatively easy to play.

The only remaining problem was that I had not hit a ball for months, let alone jump and to be honest my offensive game was in tatters. It was all a little embarrassing, me struggling away to play alongside what was obviously a class act. I was absolutely shit. Tristan was very patient however, but my demons were coming back to haunt me. I could see other players looking at Tristan and thinking they could definitely win some tournaments with him. We had only trained three times and already my lack of form was a serious concern. Grant must have been on the one hand a bit embarrassed about advising Tristan to team up with me and on the other pissing himself laughing at the fact the big Australian had as much chance of winning on the tour as a pair of non-volleyball playing pigmies from the planet no-volleyball.

Following session three Tristan simply said that everything was fine and he would be teaming up with me for the whole season, regardless. It was just what I needed to hear and with that I settled down to a sponsor search. Within days I had some clothing, bags, hats and sunglasses to help Tristan feel vindicated in his decision. Then just as things began to take shape, the partnership suffered another set back, just a month from the first tournament in Barry Island.

We had arranged to meet up with and train against Mike Randall and Chris White, two players gradually travelling up the rankings. I thought that as it was such a nice Sunday morning I would pop down early to do some fishing before we trained. There can't be many people who disable themselves for two weeks as a result of fishing, but I did and I still haven't heard the last of it from the players.

I walked out to fish on one of the groynes at Bournemouth beach, something I have done hundreds of times over many years. I fished and caught nothing, something else I had done many times over the years. I spotted Mike and Chris walking down the beach towards me and began to pack up my gear so I could go and help set up the nets. I walked along the groynes with fishing rod in one hand and bag in the other as I reached the end of the groin I had two choices, speed up and jump off the concrete over the surf and down onto the sand or duck under the railings and wander onto the beach. Choosing the former I picked up my pace and put my take off foot down to launch myself over the surf. My foot hit some green slimy weed and I went straight up in the air. My legs came up over my head and I was completely unable to control my descent.

On the side of the groynes are nasty, barnacle encrusted concrete pillars which jut out into the sea. I hit one of these and on reflection I was lucky. I had no control over my fall and could have hit my head on the concrete. It didn't feel that lucky at the time and I came down on the concrete shin first then flipping over like a rag doll and landing square on a concrete edge with my coccyx. I bent my rod (Oh! young man), which probably took some of the impact and the wind was knocked right out of me. I floundered in the surf doing a kind of mental check of my bodyparts and gasping for breath. A passer-by ran over to me a helped me to stand, saying "Bloody Hell mate, you just did a somersault!" Which was nice. I limped up to Mike and Chris who were laughing naturally, but still concerned. I thought I was going to be all right to train, but as the pain kicked in I realised I was pretty badly hurt. My back was agony and stiffening up all the time and I had a pain in my shin. I took my tracksuit bottoms off to check the damage and to my horror there was blood running down my shin bone. Mike and Chris were now more concerned.

I cleaned the cut up which was two inches long and clearly went through to my shin bone. I then limped back to my car to drive home, still in agony and still bleeding. I should have gone to hospital for stitches, but I was in a lot of pain so I doctored myself at home, painkillers, a glass of scotch and some steri-strips, just like on Doctor Quinn medicine woman. The wound wasn't a pretty sight. Then later that day I was forced to phone Tristan to confess my 'extreme fishing' injury. He tried to sound concerned and I suppose, in between the stifled laughter, he made a reasonably good effort.

Another few weeks passed before we finally got to do some real training. A week out from the first tournament, a warm-up event in Barry Island, we were just about ready to play. The one slight problem we had identified with our massed coaching skills and experience was the fact that we still hadn't recorded our first win in a training game.

So I headed into season 2000 with my sixth beach volleyball partner, in the knowledge that this was maybe going to be my last real chance to win a Grand Prix event. Five Grand Prix finals and five losses was admittedly bugging me and despite all that volleyball has given me I was still desperate to win a national event before calling it a day.

Barry Island was the first real test of this new partnership and ten seasons beach experience teaches you to prepare for some difficult situations when your seemingly perfect team gets under pressure. We performed well at the tournament taking second place and losing to Tim and Grant, 15-10.

I have generally been lucky with beach partners, but Tristan and I work really well on court. The arrangements suit both of us fine. I get the sponsorship gear and he hits the ball hard, really hard.

Bournemouth was the next tournament and our first tough test. Not only were the regular players there, but three additional Australians showed up to take wild cards. I have to admit that seeing so many good players around got to me and as a result, my usual doubts about my game surfaced. Tristan was also suffering badly, with a virus, he was more unwell than he was letting on. In game two we were well beaten by Mike Randal and Chris White and the long climb back through the losers bracket, on a hot day, finished us off. By the time we reached the last game versus the No.2 seeds Danny and Greg we were tired and went down 15-3, crashing out of the tournament in seventh place. On the positive side there were no recriminations, no histrionics, just genuine disappointment.

Tristan took some time off to get well and get fit for Poole, the next tournament. It was a fairly shaky two weeks, where small defenders with side-out hang-ups (me) can get pretty twitchy about hanging on to partners. If I had been in the States on the AVP tour I would have been very jumpy indeed. But, true to his word Tristan stuck with me and we showed up to Poole for another shot. It was clear just how ill Tristan had been at Bournemouth. The first two games at Poole were a reminder of just how good a player he is. The main change being a resumption of blocking hostilities at the net. He gets a lot of height on his block and unlike so many other blockers he has great timing, varying when he jumps to cover what the hitter is doing.

Gary Duncan, one of the funniest men on the beach really hit the nail on the head, or in my case tapped the nail gently on the head, when he summed up defence behind his partner Anthony Robert's not inconsiderable leap in a T.V interview in 1998.

"I must say" said Gary in his precise Scottish tones, smiling laconically. " It does help the defensive situation when your partner is able to eclipse the sun with his block."

Without question I now know what Gary means. It is great. Tristan jumps to block and my defensive job becomes straight forward. I find the bit of court that still has sun on it and I stand there.

It was clear early on at Poole that we were playing well, the reward? A third match on Saturday against my ex-partner Clayton, still a good friend, and his new team mate Morph. Another of those interesting little side-shows that the tour throws up. You couldn't get away from it, as we warmed up for the game Clayton and myself were tight, Morph was also affected because he was the new partner and the pressure was on him to perform. The only player not involved with the psychological ramifications of who was going to what to whom was Tristan, pretty much oblivious to the history behind the game. It wasn't that I hadn't told him, because I had. Looking back I had probably bored the pants off him with previous partner stories. He's just got a really bad memory.

It was a strange game. Clayton and Morph had barely played together and Morph had done almost no training because of his European Cup involvement with England. To be fair Tristan and I with only one training session in two weeks were not exactly a well oiled machine either. The game was bizarre and almost a non-event. Clayton hit a lot of balls straight onto my defence, we served well and Morph contributed a number of mistakes. It was all over before we knew it, 15-2 to me and Tristan. Clayton and Morph bounced straight back though, showing their mental toughness by taking Danny and Greg apart in the last game of the day, a stunning 15-1. Posting their intentions for the remainder of the tournament.

In the Sunday semi-final we ended up against a new Swedish team on the tour Vivaldi and Link, a team that had experience of professional beach volleyball on the Spanish tour. Something was clicking with myself and Tristan though and we rolled the Swede's over with a convincing 15-4 win. My fifth Grand Prix Final, a fifth chance to win an event and then back to earth with a bump. Another chance to play Tim and Grant, visions of the 15-0 Margate drubbing flooded my head.

Tristan and I sat down to watch the other semi-final Clayton and Morph versus Grant and Tim. We could not believe what we were watching, Clayton and Morph were playing with no pressure and working like a pairing with several seasons experience behind them, not just several games. So often Tim and Grant get themselves out of an indifferent start with some great serving, but Clayton and Morph were not going to let this one go and marched on to take the game 15-12. Their first tournament, their first final.

I have to admit, with no pride whatsoever that the half hour period following that result was a mental roller coaster ride for me. I should have been happy, Tim and Grant out the way and a chance to play the team we had demolished the day before for the title. Sport doesn't work like that though and before I knew it I was a slave to some very negative lateral thinking. Clayton and Morph, relaxed, already achieved a place in the final. Me, 33 years old, maybe my last chance to win a Grand Prix event. The previous game against Clayton had been a non-event, we barely got any information to work with, because they barely did anything. Clayton's chance for revenge in front of witnesses and because of the brutality of sport, his chance to say "You see, you never had it in you to win one." Not that he would ever have said that, out loud.

I worked hard to concentrate and collect my thoughts gradually steering my mind back to the fact I was just about to walk out on court with a former World Series player as a partner to play against a couple of players I had coached over the last year and who's games I knew really well.

As a defender you quickly learn what your best weapons are. Grant and I may not be the fastest boys around the sand, but something watching Grant over the years has taught me is to know your opponent. If you stand in the right place to start with then you considerably reduce the amount of movement involved and force your opponent to play shots they don't normally play, leading to mistakes. Watch learn and remember.

I stood in the players tent just gazing out over the sea and gradually turning my thoughts to positive images of making defensive touches. Then it just popped into my head, probably the most devastating thought I could have had. It floated around unchallenged, this is my best chance to win one......ever. I was disturbed from my thought by a tap on the shoulder. "I know what your thinking and you should stop thinking it" said Grant.

"Oh Yeh! what am I thinking ?" I replied.

"You're thinking, this is my best chance.......ever." He said quietly, then raised his eyebrows and wandered out of the tent.

Over the seasons Grant has repeatedly called it right and that is why I think he is one of the best coaches I have ever met, a potential that has yet to be utilised properly in this country. He has an ability to see things really well both on and off court. His comment was what I needed to hear. At Bournemouth he had reminded me of what I was capable of when I was looking at all the other talented players doing their stuff at the tournament. Here at Poole I was just about to play a couple of his best mates in the final, he didn't have to say anything.

So we went onto court and from the warm-up it was clear Clayton and Morph had shaken off any crap from the previous day. In the first phases of the game they were strong, serving well, blocking well and for Morph's part making it almost impossible to get the ball on the sand without him touching it. They led 6-3 and latterly 8-5, but we scraped hard and brought the score back to 8-7. That was the turning point and although I contributed some good work in back court it was Tristan who really picked up the pace on serve and block. We breezed past them to set up match point and then as usual couldn't finish. You know the routine, dreams of making an ace for the win or getting a swing for the title. We got those chances and missed them. It was left to Morph to roll an easy shot out over the sideline.

As Morph hit the shot I watched it and began to chase it down. It looked out, but I think I was going to play it, if I got there. It was the first time in weeks I had been happy with my immobility, I pulled up short and just watched as the ball dropped onto the sand, missing the sideline by inches. That was it, the quest was over, I had won a Grand Prix tournament. I shouted loud, it was finally after ten seasons, in the 'tick off things to do in life' bag.

The season went from strength to strength. Tristan is a great partner to play with. He takes care of his own business and doesn't get involved with yours, save to offer some words of encouragement here and there. Too many players, while not taking care of their own inadequacies, feel they should spend time addressing their partners. Yes, hands up everyone, me as well. Playing alongside Tristan I get to relax about my beach shortfalls and concentrate almost entirely on what has kept me in the top five for ten seasons, namely my partners (see there I go again.)

Season 2000 has been a fantastic one, my best yet. We even recorded a 12-2; 12-10 win over Grant and Tim in the Brighton Invitational event. That just about completes the picture. With Tristan as a partner I have achieved more than I expected and probably more than I deserved. In time honoured tradition though, give it a few weeks and I will probably hate the big headed Aussie git.

I have spent a few weeks, after success at the Poole tournament, sauntering around events and telling people I had now lost my edge, due to that win. The win gave me a new feeling of confidence on court and lifted the pressure of wanting to win one. Tristan and myself have made every final since then. At Margate (lost 15-3 to Tim and Grant), Brighton (already mentioned, although tempting to mention it again for old time's sake), Weymouth (lost 15-10 from 10-5 up, no need to dwell there) and the British Championships (lost in three sets 12-4; 4-12; 10-15). Probably my fondest memory, after the win at Poole, and one of my proudest moments, was when I was presented with the 'player of the tournament' award at Weymouth this year. An award that I have coveted for so long having seen other players collect it. I went up to receive the trophy and many memories came flooding back, from my first steps on the Weymouth sand, to what I felt might be my last game at Weymouth. Thank you to the Weymouth lads, Graeme, Steve, and Pete for that.

That's all folks............................?

The last scheduled Grand Prix tournament of the season was Boscombe, my last event. Tristan and I had found little time to practice in the previous two weeks, but had still kept in good shape. We won through the first two rounds, 15-6 against Peter and Keith Barker and 15-10 against a really good Swedish 'wild card' team. This set up a tough third match against Danny and Greg. Danny and Greg played very well and we went down 12-15 in a close game, which left us in a fifth place game versus Gary Duncan and Anthony Roberts (two other players bowing out after years in the game), a game scheduled for Sunday morning. The winners of the game progressed to semi-final tie against Grant and Tim.

Heading off to bed at 10.45pm on the Saturday night I had a phone call from Gary to tell me that he and Anthony had withdrawn from the event, they had informed the organisers and therefore our 9.00am game was a walkover. Gary was calling out of courtesy so that Tristan and I didn't bust a gut to get to the court at 9.00am for a game that was not going ahead.

Unfortunately, I took this phone call at face value. I hadn't anticipated that many seasons on the Grand prix tour, over sixty beach volleyball tournaments (never late once), service as a magazine writer, coach, commentator, tournament organiser, player negotiator and commission member would ll count for nothing in the final analysis. Tristan and I arrived at 9.20am to find that Gary and Anthony had left an answerphone message with an event co-ordinator who was not attending on the Sunday. Although many were aware that they had pulled out of the event, as had the Swedish team of Link and Vivaldi (it transpired) nobody present seemed to be able to clarify why there were no teams on the beach for the two non-existent 9.00am games. The beach commission made a decision, driven largely, it seemed, by justifiable anger at the withdrawal of the two sets of players.

Without listening to any evidence from myself or from Clayton Lucas, the other party affected by the withdrawal, all four teams were disqualified from the tournament. In light of the fact that this was widely known to be my last competitive day on the sand I was upset to find that those in charge believed that I would jeopardise my final games on the British Tour by simply turning up late. It was a disappointing and very sobering moment and at that point I realised just how tired I felt after fifteen years. Devoid of any inclination to fight for what others considered of little value I made my peace with the decision makers and left the beach. I was denied the opportunity to do what I had planned to do for some months, to go out as I came in playing as hard as I could, complaining about ref's decisions and generally looking miserable.

I was absolutely devastated by the events of that morning, my wish to play a last couple of games on centre court and retire with some dignity overshadowed by the need to find scapegoats. The players that were punished were the players that actually showed up. You can quote event rules and player agreements at me and I'll agree with you all the way. The regulations need to be tightened. The fact is though that when I needed people that I had known for many years, to take five minutes, five minutes that I think I had earned, to organise their thoughts and consider the evidence in a rational manner, it didn't happen. We were in the wrong place at quite literally the wrong time. Sunday morning's ruling was recended at 5.30pm that day in a phone call from Richard Cannon and some apologies were made, unfortunately all too late.

If this is to be the end, apart from the last event cock-up, I honestly couldn't have wished for more. If I had been writing it, I would have written it almost exactly like this and that makes it even more special. A good finish in the indoor league, an indoor Cup Final and my best season ever on the beach, with a former World Series player. A player that just the other day happened to say "So what are your plans for next summer, Simon ?"

It's a proud moment when people pay you compliments on your game and it is so rewarding to establish yourself in the sport of your choice. For me the most rewarding elements of my playing career have come from the fact that it was never really on the cards and maybe that makes it mean more, because I worked hard to earn it. I will retire with only one objective unachieved, my schoolboy dream to play for England. A dream that would have enabled me to improve as a player through contact with a World class coach like Jefferson Williams.

I started late, at eighteen, I was never big and I never really had a huge leap. Talent wise I have the same genetics as the majority of players reading this book and far less talent than many, many others.

I have enjoyed playing with you, against you, coaching you and being coached by you, over the years. We have all travelled the miles and paid the money. One day, as I have discovered, the playing will stop. If you still have a few years left in you get out there and do it, I'll be watching and enjoying.

Most of us put ourselves through it all because we love to play, but let's make no bones here, all of us do it because sometimes, just sometimes, we get to win.